The Last Love Letter

3 Keys to Living with
Joy, Peace, and Purpose

By

DeAnne Joy, LCSW
Transformation & Legacy Coach

Foreword by: Marwa Kilani, M.D.

DEDICATION

To my parents, Vern and Judy, who both left this physical planet much too soon. I am proud to embrace the name you gifted to me that embodies who I Am. The gifts you gave me, both in life and in your deaths, are profound and life-changing. Because of you, I found my strength, vulnerability, compassion, resilience, commitment, and authentic voice. I found my passion, my purpose, and my Joy. Because of you, I am changed for good. Continue to remind me of your constant presence in my life. I am blessed to have had you as my parents in life and now as my Angels for eternity.

Table of Contents

FOREWORD

Alles hat ein Ende, nur die Wurst hat zwei

All things have one end… except a sausage… which has two.

-- Old German saying

I first met DeAnne several years ago when she came to work at Providence Holy Cross as a clinical social worker covering the oncology unit, where the majority of the patients were undergoing some of the most grueling of medical treatments. In her role as social worker, DeAnne completed assessments and developed coping strategies with each of these patients, considering the complexities they faced. One imperative message she sought to teach each of her patients, as well as their loved ones, was the importance of living in the moment and experiencing life to its fullest.

Working alongside DeAnne, I found myself completely immersed in her deep insight and guidance. She empowered each of her patients to take control of their lives, define their wishes, and find joy in each day. When DeAnne contacted me many years later, inviting me to write the foreword to this book, I reflected on the many encounters we experienced together, as well as the numerous patients that passed through our doors, some prepared for dying, while others struggled to the end.

As a palliative care doctor, I work with patients and their families suffering from the most serious of illnesses. The likelihood of death is real and palpable for most of these individuals. It is very true that not every palliative care patient will experience immediate and imminent death, but the reality holds that death is inevitable, and the better prepared these individuals and their families are, the less amounts of suffering may be observed.

It doesn't seem to matter, man or woman, Christian, Jewish, Muslim or Buddhist, young or old, each individual suffers differently, experiencing anxiety at varying degrees. What I have learned over the years of palliating thousands of patients is that no two patients are the same nor will they experience their disease process, joys, and grief during their time of illness in the same way.

Meeting "Heinrich" affirmed the fact that, regardless of where a patient is in their journey, meaning can be made out of the experience. Heinrich, an 89-year-old German man, came to our hospital for complications related to his metastatic lung cancer treatment. One would assume that, given the severity of his disease state, his age, and how he suffered, that he would have been terrified of where he was at and the potential death facing him eye-to-eye. But in fact, quite the opposite was true.

Not only was he jovial, but he shared this very poignant German saying - *Alles hat ein Ende, nur die Wurst hat zwei* – "All things have one end, except for German sausages with two ends," he translated! He laughed so hard it was heard throughout the oncology unit! Our team not only joined in his laughter, but later returned throughout the days to take part in his recanting of his life in Germany and the U.S.

He wanted to discuss his end-of-life healthcare options with us, as he shared his only worries surrounding the potential to suffer needlessly. He reflected on the German idiom and recognized his inevitable end. We had deep discussions on what made life meaningful for him, with his avowal that only time with his wife was worth living for. Yet, he wanted to do so comfortably, and not within the confines of a hospital room.

Together, we completed his health care advance directive and documentation of his wishes so that any health care provider could reflect on his words prior to the initiation of any treatments that might cause conflict. His wife would never have to wonder what his desires were, allowing for a peaceful end when the time came. He left the hospital to continue his treatment, but more importantly, to spend quality time with his wife. Heinrich's focus was not on dying; it was on enjoying his life as completely as possible.

So unless you're a German sausage, remember that all things must come to an end. As you read through

DeAnne's book, reflect on your own life, your relationships, and what makes your life meaningful. Yes, death is certain, and for some it may be scary, but it doesn't have to be. Focus on what is most important: family, love, friendships, career, blue skies. Live each day of your life to the fullest so that, like Heinrich, whenever your inevitable end comes, you and your loved ones can be at peace.

There is much that surrounds you to bring you joy. Now go out and seek it.

Marwa Kilani, M.D., M.B.A.
Medical Director, Palliative Care
Providence Holy Cross Medical Center
Mission Hills, California

INTRODUCTION

Spoiler Alert. We're ALL gonna die. Yes, even you.

Precisely 100% of us are going to die at some point. That is a certainty. Yet, we tend to walk through life as though our time here is infinite.

My name is DeAnne Joy. I'm a transformation and legacy expert, also known as *the Midlife Reboot Mentor^{TM}*. I teach people how to live each day FULLY, leave a legacy that MATTERS, and **live** that legacy NOW. My superpower is helping driven women in midlife discover joy, peace, and purpose after they've been knocked off their feet by the pain of a loss or life-changing event.

We all have our own wake-up calls that force us to really look at how we are living our lives. Mine came five years ago when my mother, a healthy, full-of-life, vibrant 68-year-old, took a horrific fall down her basement stairs onto a concrete floor. She suffered massive head and brain trauma that left her in a coma. A day and a half later, she was removed from life support.

What I know for sure is that **we are not born with an expiration date stamped on the bottom of our feet.** Life can change on a dime and tomorrow simply isn't promised.

Death is a difficult topic for many of us to wrap our heads around and explore; often we fear or avoid discussing it openly. Fortunately, this concern is beginning to shift as the palliative care and hospice movements grow, which I will talk more about in the chapters ahead. The medical, spiritual, and legal arenas are providing more education around the importance of completing advance healthcare directives, which are written documents that explain your healthcare wishes should you ever become incapacitated or unable to speak for yourself.

I've dealt with my own personal experiences with death and loss that have shaped my outlook on life, which you'll learn more about in the chapters ahead. I also draw on my professional experience as a licensed clinical therapist and end-of-life social worker for more than two decades. Having trained physicians and other health care providers in facilitating end-of-life conversations with patients and their families, I am a strong advocate for completing advance healthcare directives to prepare for the future, while fully embracing life today. I will share more about the role that my mother's advance directive, which I refer to as her "last love letter," played in how my family and I were able to experience her death.

A large part of my work's mission is to elevate a conscious, dignified, life-affirming conversation about life and death. For me, the real question is, "What would life be like if, instead of fearing or avoiding death, we used it as our gauge for how we are living TODAY?"

What if we lived from a place of accepting that we are ALL going to die at some point, and we lived each day as though it could be our last, knowing that tomorrow simply isn't promised?

What if we lived each day asking ourselves the questions:

- If today were my last day in this physical world, would I be happy with who I was and how I showed up in the world?

- Did I live fully and go for my dreams and desires?

- Did I live my life fully and love deeply?

- Is there anything that I need resolution on to be at peace today?

- Did I share my gifts with the world?

How would you live your life differently if you lived each day from **that** place?

Would you...
- Live more authentically?

- Experience more joy, peace, and fulfillment?

- Live your life full-out, with NO REGRETS?

- Let go of old beliefs, habits, and patterns that no longer serve you?

- Reach for your dreams?

- Give and receive love deeply?

- Make an impact on the planet and leave a legacy that makes a difference?

What TRULY matters to you? What do you need to let go of in order to go for your dreams? What do you need to **believe** and who do you need to be **now** in order to achieve your goals and dreams so that you can look back at the end of your life, whenever that time comes, with **no regrets?**

Death is as real and natural a part of life as birth. And, yes, we are ALL going to die. It is not a mystery. It is not an unknown. It is a basic fact. We just don't have a crystal ball to let us know when that time will come. Death is not morbid, and it doesn't have to be frightening; it's simply a part of life, just as birth is a part of life.

Until we fully accept that our own death is real, natural, and inevitable, we cannot FULLY embrace life. It is only when we come to an awareness that our time on this physical earth is finite, that we begin to live each day with greater urgency, intention, and purpose. It gives us the opportunity to be authentically present and to appreciate each moment, each experience, and each relationship.

The gift that my parents gave me, both in life and in their deaths, is clarity about my purpose: to teach people about the importance of completing advance healthcare directives to prepare for the future, while fully embracing life **today**. To love deeply, live boldly, share our gifts, and leave this world with NO REGRETS. Most importantly, I am here to teach people to not just leave their legacy after they die, but rather to **LIVE their legacy NOW.**

This book is about is about creating a candid, uplifting conversation about living AND dying. It is about seeing death as a part of life, as the spiritual and transformational experience that dying can be. Ultimately though, this book is about awakening to your own life, no longer fearing or avoiding death, but instead using it as a gauge for how you are living life today. It is about living each day FULLY, enjoying life, loving and connecting deeply, and recognizing that we are all meant for something bigger, that there is a contribution that we are meant to make in our time on this earth. Most of all, this book is about living with no regrets.

I don't know about you, but I don't want to get to the end of my life with my dreams and gifts still inside of me. I don't want to look back at my life with regrets. And I don't want that for you either.

This book is not meant to be an all-encompassing course on how to live life fully with no regrets. **My 12-week coaching program, *Ultimate Midlife Reboot: Living with No Regrets*** [TM], teaches women in midlife how to live fully, love deeply, and share the gifts they were meant to share. I couldn't possibly cover all of that information here; that would do you a disservice. There isn't a shortcut for doing the work necessary to create the life that you want and deserve. Beyond this book, you can start with my free video mini-course, *3 Keys to Discovering YOU in Midlife,* which you can find at deanne-joy.com/3-keys-book-gift/.

This book is meant to help you learn how to:

- Live each day FULLY with joy, peace, and power

- Recognize that YOU are in the driver's seat of your life and YOU decide how it turns out

- Love you as you are, flaws and all, and decide what makes you truly HAPPY

- Apply specific tools and strategies for living the life you desire and DESERVE

- Get off the deferred life-plan and get EXCITED about life again!

- Shift your understanding of death so that you embrace your life fully and live each day with NO REGRETS

- Understand the essentials of advance care planning and PREPARE your healthcare advance directive so that your loved ones never face the burden of making difficult decisions on your behalf

- Know that you are meant for something BIGGER – that you have a contribution to make!

- Begin your journey of EVOLUTION so that you can get to your CONTRIBUTION

- Leave a legacy that makes a DIFFERENCE on the planet

We dive much deeper into all these topics in my transformational coaching programs. For more information about my programs or coaching with me, visit: deanne-joy.com/work-with-me/.

So many people want to live their lives joyfully, abundantly, and with no regrets, yet they want to skip the work necessary to do that. They want to leave their legacy without doing the work to **live** their legacy now. They want to complete their healthcare advance directive without fully understanding their own values, beliefs, and wishes, or without having conversations with their loved ones.

I know that after reading this book, you'll **want** to do that work, and you'll see the value it will bring, not only to your life, but to the lives of those you love.

You'll have no excuse NOT to create the life you want - a life filled with joy, peace, and purpose!

If you...

- have been knocked off your feet by your own wake-up call in life

- have a yearning in your heart

- have spent far too much of your life putting everyone and everything else first

- have been unable or unwilling to release past hurts and resentment

- crave deeper connections with yourself and those you love

- desire a deeper sense of meaning and fulfillment

- are no longer willing to settle for less than you deserve and are capable of

- have waited to start living the life that is truly possible for you

- are "okay," but not **overflowing** or "fine," but not **fabulous**

Consider the possibility that there is a reason that you found your way to this book. As you continue through the chapters that follow, you will be offered a different lens through which to see your life, actionable tools and strategies, and perhaps even the clarity you seek.

The first step is simply to make a **decision.**

What if today was your last? **Would you have lived FULLY, loved DEEPLY, and shared the gifts you were meant to share?**

As cliché as it is, live each day as though it could be your last.

Because one day, it WILL be.

PART I

LESSONS IN LIVING AND DYING

Early Loss

I am a 15-year old sophomore in high school and I've just been dropped off in front of my school after a doctor's appointment. As I am walking up to the school, I hear a car incessantly blasting its horn. I turn around to see what all the commotion is to find my aunt waving me down and yelling at me to come quickly.

As a too-cool-for-school teenager, I casually walk to the car, not wanting to appear too eager to run over to my aunt, just in case any of my classmates might catch a glimpse of me. Of course, I cannot possibly know the gravity of the situation I am about to step into. As I get closer to the car, I can see that my aunt is crying hysterically, telling me to hurry up and get in the car.

I jump in to find that several of my relatives, including my brother, are already in the car. Little do I know that my life is about to be turned completely upside-down by tragedy. Everyone is crying and upset, and I hear someone say that something has happened with my dad and that they don't know if he is going to make it.

It is a 50-minute ride to the hospital where my dad is, but feels like an eternity. I am thinking the whole ride that this all seems a bit dramatic and surely he will be just fine when we get there. I simply cannot entertain the thought of him not making it.

My dad, who was 39 at the time, underwent a routine surgery to remove two abdominal hernias. Back in 1985, unlike today, this routine surgery required several days in the hospital. My parents had divorced a few years earlier, so my brothers and I visited my dad the day after surgery, without my mom. He looked good, was his usual, joking, gregarious self and was scheduled to be discharged home the next day.

On the day he was supposed to be released from the hospital, my dad developed a blood clot that went to his lung (a pulmonary embolism), causing him to go into cardiac arrest. When his heart stopped, CPR was administered and he regained a heartbeat. He went into cardiac arrest for a second time, and once again was resuscitated successfully, only this time, he was without oxygen to the brain for nearly 25 minutes while undergoing CPR.

A lack of oxygen for nearly 25 minutes is an incredibly long time; brain damage begins to occur after less than four minutes without oxygen. After more than 20 minutes, catastrophic brain injury is almost a certainty. Had my father been older, the medical team probably would not have continued CPR for so long. But because he was only 39, and otherwise generally healthy, they didn't want to give up. While they were able to revive him, he was unconscious and unable to breathe on his own, likely suffering severe brain damage. Anyone who knew my father would know that he would absolutely **never** want to be kept alive in such a state.

My dad was a loud, charismatic, outgoing sports fiend. At the age of 29, he lost his arm below the elbow in an accident. Even with one arm, he was an exceptional bowler and golfer, winning awards and tournaments. If he'd had the opportunity to discuss his wishes with anyone or complete his own advance directive, he would have undoubtedly said, "Don't ever keep me alive like that; just pull the plug." He would have said it as bluntly as that, but with an expletive or two for emphasis.

But he never had the opportunity to make his wishes known. First, it probably never even occurred to him to complete an advance directive because he was so young. And, second, he was not the kind of guy to discuss things like death, anyway.

Because there was no advance directive and my parents had divorced several years earlier, my grandparents were considered the next of kin to make decisions on my dad's behalf. My dad was my grandmother's oldest living son. He was her boy, even at 39. She was absolutely heartbroken at the thought of losing him. I cannot imagine that she would have been able to make the decision to remove him from life-support, which could very well have left him in a permanent vegetative state (a coma). Thankfully, she didn't have to make that decision, as he ended up going into a third cardiac arrest and did not survive.

We finally arrive at the hospital after what feels like hours in the car. I spend the whole ride convincing myself that everyone is overreacting and that my dad is fine. We are taken to a little meeting room where my aunt is comforting my grandmother as she looks up at us, voice cracking, and says, "They couldn't save him."

"Wait. He was fine yesterday. He was supposed to come home today. Did this really just happen?" I think to myself as I stand there, stunned.

Most of the rest of that day is a blur. It is several hours before my mom arrives at the hospital. I am sitting alone on the floor in a hallway with my head down when I hear her voice call my name. When I look up and see her coming down the hall, I immediately run into her arms and completely melt.

Over the years, through my work as a social worker and therapist in end-of-life care, I witnessed many situations with patients and families in which family members had an agonizing time with even the thought of considering letting their loved one go, even when the prognosis for any meaningful recovery was grim. I often considered, what would have happened had my father not suffered another cardiac arrest? Would my grandparents have been able to make the decision to remove life support? Would he have ended up in a vegetative state? Every time I consider that possibility, I thank God that he went on his own, and that those were not decisions that had to be wrestled with.

I believe it would have killed my grandmother emotionally and spiritually to have to let her son go or to be the one to have to make that choice. I truly don't think she could have lived with that decision; it would have been a cross that she would have had to bear until her own death. I think my dad knew that, and allowed himself to go. As searingly painful as his death was, I am grateful that he died on his own. The alternative would have been far more unbearable.

For many years, my perspective of my dad's life was viewed through the lens of his death; this movie, this story, of what happened on 'that day'. The sadness of it, my grief and the teenage acting-out that followed, the impact that it had on my life, all the events that he missed: high school parents' nights, athletic events, high-school and college graduations. My memories of my dad's life were overwhelmed by the reality of his death. When I spoke of him, it was from the perspective of having lost him at the age of 15. I just didn't know how else to process it. The grief that I carried was unresolved for a long time. In fact, it wasn't even something that I, or the people that cared about me, recognized as grief.

It wasn't only the grief of losing my dad that lingered. There were also issues that were unresolved from my childhood that involved him. My dad was a loving guy who had his own inner demons. At times, he struggled with drinking and had violent outbursts, typically targeted toward my mom. I had a chaotic upbringing and it was difficult for me as a kid to understand the dichotomy that my dad was. This gregarious, outgoing, charismatic, loving guy could also become angry, violent, and frightening, especially when he drank. The grief of my earlier life with him went unresolved along with his death.

It wasn't until I was in college, studying for my bachelor's degree in Social Work, with the goal of becoming a therapist and working with troubled teens like I had been, that I finally started to heal the grief and woundedness that I carried for all those years. That healing came out of my own struggles with substance abuse, depression, chaotic relationships, and suicidal thoughts. Right after graduation from college, I checked myself into an inpatient substance-abuse treatment center.

I had no idea how intense the treatment would be, but it was like having 20 years of therapy in a span of just 28 days. During treatment was the first time that I was able to simply see my dad as a perfectly imperfect human being who was on his own journey, doing the best that he knew how to do, when his life came to an abrupt end. For the first time, I realized that my parents, like me, were simply human beings. They were fallible and vulnerable. They had their own struggles, dreams, failures, desires, dark sides, accomplishments, and strengths.

After years of heartache and turmoil, I was actually able to celebrate the life that my dad lived, rather than grieve the one day that he died. I was able to recognize and acknowledge the gifts that he blessed me with, both in life and in death. I decided to honor the qualities that I most loved about him by taking them on myself. I admired his gritty charisma and ability to make people laugh at themselves. By taking on those qualities of his (minus the crassness), I was able to lighten up and not take myself or others too seriously.

The decision to celebrate the life that my dad lived rather than grieve the day he died was a life-changing shift in healing and perspective for me. That choice forever changed my understanding of and relationship to death. The idea that it is not necessary for us to live perpetually in our grief was a huge awakening for me. I realized that it is actually a disservice to the person who died when we focus on their death rather than on the whole life that they lived. I learned that it is ok to recognize the gifts that they give us, both in their lives and through their deaths. We can choose to carry those gifts forward with us and they can change the entire trajectory of our lives. Taking on the qualities of those that we most admire and making them our own is also a powerful way to honor them.

That is not to say that experiencing our loss and grief isn't necessary. It is. As a society, we have just as much trouble being open about grief as we do with talking about death. We don't want to ignore the grief process, but we also want to move through it rather than become paralyzed by it. One of the things that can help us to move through grief is to acknowledge the pain of the loss, while also celebrating the gifts and the lessons that we received from our loved ones and through their passing.

Another life-changing awareness that I gained through my dad's death was an understanding of the circle of life. My younger sister, Catie, turned a year old on the day my dad was buried. Her birth and life literally saved four broken teenagers, me and my three older brothers, in a way that nothing or no one else could have healed. She was, and continues to be, an incredible gift in my life and one of my most precious earth angels. She symbolizes the circle of life. As one life moves from the physical to the Spirit world, another proceeds from the Spirit world to the physical.

Tomorrow Isn't Promised

With the early life experience of losing my dad, I have always had a keen sense of how life can change on a dime. I became acquainted with death at a young age and came to see it as a part of life. At first, I didn't see the gift and the beauty in it, but as I grew, I came to feel more comfortable with it and viewed it as a natural occurrence. Not that the circumstances around it were always "natural," but I saw it as an inevitable certainty, and not in a bad way.

Where I grew up in the U.S., we seem to have a societal fear of death, as though if we talk about it, we might somehow hasten it. We know that dying is inevitable, yet we fear, avoid, or deny our own mortality. We try not to think about death; we grieve others' losses and feel lucky that it wasn't us, at least until we are faced with our own loss.

I'm not sure exactly where this collective discomfort with death comes from. Maybe it's because advancing medicine allows us to live longer and longer lives, creating the illusion that death is far off. Or maybe our discomfort comes from seeing the elderly forgotten and isolated, which makes us feel afraid that it could also happen to us. Or maybe it's simply the fear of the unknown and uncertainty about what happens after we die.

I believe that our fear comes from a combination of all of those things, but I also believe that our discomfort with death comes from seeing ourselves as only our physical body, rather than as the soul energy that is housed in our physical body. I remember learning in fourth-grade science that energy never dies, it only changes form. Our physical bodies are made from pure energy, so it has always made sense to me that, when our physical body dies, the energy simply changes form.

There is a purity, connectedness, and energy of the soul that reaches far beyond the physical body. The body is simply a vessel that houses the spirit. Death is as natural as birth; in both instances, energy changes form. When we embrace that notion, and we understand that death can be a deeply profound and spiritual experience, just as birth, it isn't nearly as frightening.

Acknowledging the reality of death allows you to really awaken to your own life. It's about truly embracing this life and living it FULLY **now** – on this physical planet, in this human body. It is recognizing that we all eventually shed our mortal coil. We will all die, just as naturally as we have all been born. When we can embrace that fact, rather than be afraid of it, it allows us a new experience with both life and death. We can begin to consider the possibility that life doesn't end when we leave this physical world;

that our bodies are simply the vessels that house our souls, and when the vessel breaks down, the soul continues to live on.

When we accept that our transition from the physical world is inevitable and that it's not just the unlucky few that die, but all of us, then we can embrace the life that we live in a much more real, authentic, conscious, and awakened way. We can begin to allow life to happen, and allow ourselves to just BE, wherever we are, however we are. We can begin to let go of the attachment to the fountain of youth, keeping up with the Joneses, the constant pursuit of the "perfect" soul-mate, or hiding behind our fabulous social-media lives.

Instead, we can just accept life where it is, in all of its imperfections. We can be real. We can have honest, authentic conversations. We can be okay with the ugliness that this human experience can sometimes reveal. We can accept loss, in all its forms, as part of life. We can let go of the dream of the ideal, and simply live our lives in the best way that we know how and assume that everyone else is doing the same. We can be present in every moment, every experience - the joy, the pain, the hurt, the triumphs, the challenges, the losses, the ugly cries, the disappointments, the failures, the overcoming. All of it. When we can embrace life for ALL that it is, in all of its duality, that is where we begin to truly LIVE.

When we accept that precisely 100% of us are going to die, that death is a reality - a natural, mysterious part of life - that acceptance allows us the opportunity to tune into our life's journey and our life's purpose in a profoundly new way. We become connected to the journey of our soul. We become more deeply and authentically connected with others.

Then we are open to all of the possibilities and opportunities that exist in the moment. Then we are able to be fully present, appreciating and living in each moment, no longer concerned about the past that we cannot change, and no longer focused on the future that hasn't even happened yet. We are mindfully focused on this moment, right now, and fully present in it.

We stop trying to control, but rather allow things to just be. We allow life to simply unfold when we let go of the need to control and create experiences as we think that they "should be." We understand that life is constantly evolving, and we accept those shifts as they come. We simply flow with life as it is, trusting that there is a divine order to our lives that exists far beyond the physical body and physical world. That is where the opportunity for profound healing lies.

Critical Care

After earning my Master's Degree in Social Work at the age of 22, I began my career as a clinical therapist and worked primarily in mental health for the first decade of my career. I had back surgery when I was 28, and decided on a bit of a whim, to leave the cold climate of the upper Midwest for sunny Los Angeles. I landed a job at a large metropolitan hospital and worked in a number of areas including dialysis, ER, and Intensive Care. My role as a social worker was to act as a liaison between the medical team and patients or families, assist patients and their loved ones in coping with the illness or injury they were facing, and help patients make their healthcare wishes known.

Although my mother was one of several nurses in her family, I wasn't sure how I would like working in a medical setting, especially since I had a tendency to faint as a child at the sight of blood or even the thought of a needle. I was always the kid who would gladly - without hesitation - take the 14 days of antibiotics over the single shot. I really hated needles and I hated blood.

As it turned out, despite the reality of needles and blood, I fell in love with critical care. I loved the pace, the frenzy, the challenge, and I grew to love the miracle of medicine. The hospital I worked at was a teaching facility, which meant that I worked very closely with a constantly rotating team of interns and residents, as well as the supervising physicians. The hospital was also a tertiary facility, which meant that the sickest or most complex patients were often transferred there, as well as patients with severe traumatic brain injuries or possible brain death. It was this experience that even more deeply shaped my relationship with death and my work with end-of-life issues. Through my work, I was able to see the beauty in death, the spiritual nature of it, and the possibility of a "good death."

During my time working in critical care, I developed a pretty good knowledge about medical terminology, diagnoses, medications and interventions, brain trauma, and life-sustaining measures. As was often the case, everything moved very quickly, and the doctors had to interact with families whenever they could grab the time to speak with them about their loved ones' care. Whenever those meetings involved difficult discussions or end-of-life decisions, I was always asked to help facilitate the conversation. If I hadn't yet had the opportunity to meet them, sometimes I was pulled into those very sensitive family meetings with not much more than a 60-second summary about the situation and status of the patient.

Just a few days after starting in the ICU, I had my first experience with facilitating a conversation about end-of-life care that would become a pivotal experience in my work and life. Part of my role was to act as a liaison between patients/families and the treatment team. I checked in daily with families to make sure that they received adequate information from the treatment team, that they understood what was happening with their loved ones' care, and that they had all of their questions answered and the support they needed.

It was in this role that I introduced myself to Jill, the wife of a patient in the ICU who had been admitted for respiratory failure and placed on a ventilator. Jill's husband Gary, had end-stage lung cancer with no written advance directive, and had stayed at home until he was in significant respiratory distress. His only form of advance directive over the years had been to verbalize that he never wanted to live as a "vegetable."

The ICU attending physician and I met with Jill to discuss Gary's status and the plan of care. The physician explained Gary's condition in detail and shared that it was unlikely that he would ever be able to come off the ventilator or even leave the hospital alive.

Since this situation was a new experience for me, I was initially a bit taken aback at how blunt the doctor was, but over time I realized just how important it is for providers to be absolutely candid with their patients' loved ones. It is important, in part, because families cannot make life and death decisions on behalf of their loved ones without a clear and honest understanding of the reality of the situation. That understanding is what enables them to **really** consider what their loved one would want if they were able to speak for themselves - to step into their shoes and essentially be their mouthpiece.

Although he had expressed his wishes verbally over time, Gary did not have a formal advance directive. They had no children together and Jill was the decision-maker, as next-of-kin. Gary was an outgoing, extremely intelligent, strong-willed person. He was highly skilled in the arts of music and painting, an inventor and entrepreneur, and a successfully-published author of historical fiction.

It had become clear over the previous few months that Gary was quite ill. In spite of that, he refused to see a doctor for a long time. He had not had good experiences with healthcare providers in his life, and tended toward natural or nutritional alternatives. He always had an aversion to seeking medical care and seeing doctors. He was a lifelong smoker, until he quit seven years before his death. Still, as he became ill, he greatly feared that he might have lung cancer but continued to avoid a diagnosis by not making doctor's appointments or addressing the obvious health issues.

By the time it was confirmed that he did indeed have lung cancer, there were no treatment options available. Still, he avoided discussing how ill he might actually be. Like many others that I have encountered in my years of working with the ill and dying, he was averse to even considering the possibility of death, let alone discussing it or exploring his wishes. Perhaps he believed that if he didn't acknowledge death as a possibility, that it wouldn't happen; or conversely, that if he *did* think about it, that he would somehow hasten his own death.

With his aversion to traditional medicine, he made it very clear to his wife that he did not want to die in a hospital and did not want to become a "vegetable." By the time he was brought to the hospital, he was in respiratory distress and quickly lapsed into full respiratory failure. However, he was willing to accept being on a ventilator, **if** there was a possibility that he could recover and go home.

Unfortunately, he was never able to come off of the ventilator. He was in the hospital for an entire month. Jill tried to do everything that she felt was possible to honor his wishes. Gary felt that, if he had the proper nutrition, he could recover. So, Jill pursued every avenue that she could to advocate for her husband, even bringing in a lip-reading specialist to try to help her husband communicate his wishes through the breathing tube.

She had alternative nutritional supplements brought in and administered to him. She tried everything. As many do, Jill kept herself extremely busy "doing" and being in action; so much so, that she allowed little time for herself to just grieve her husband's clearly declining health or address her own guilt for feeling that she should have pushed the issue of treatment more with him and forced him to see a doctor sooner.

By the time it became clear that Gary was not going to recover, his wish was to go home, even if he were to die there. Again, Jill did everything she could to honor her husband's wishes, in spite of the limits in practicality and warnings from the medical team that he would not survive even the ride home. Finally, she realized that she had explored and done everything she could to honor his wish to try to return home, and she chose to stop pursuing the alternative treatments.

Gary passed away in the middle of the night while Jill had gone home to get some rest. As many loved ones do, Jill questioned whether she should have gone home, whether it was "selfish" to leave. I have seen dozens and dozens of times when the dying person waited for everyone to leave before they let go. Knowing what I learned about Gary, my intuition was that he would not allow himself to die while Jill was there, knowing how difficult it would be for her.

I felt such empathy for Jill and I could not imagine being in her situation, having to make these kinds of decisions on behalf of a loved one. I thought about what it would feel like to deal with a sudden life-threatening illness, but then on top of that, to have to make decisions about life-support that could affect your loved ones' quality of life, for the rest of their lives. Jill was so full of guilt and second-guessing, questioning whether she had done 'enough.' Could she have given him more comfort; could she have touched him, massaged him; could she have been at the hospital more? She prayed that she had done all that her husband wanted.

In retrospect, Jill wished that Gary's primary care doctor had discussed palliative care and hospice options with them, feeling that one of these options would have better achieved Gary's wishes for his end-of-life care. The focus of palliative care is managing the symptoms of illness and providing relief from pain, while the illness can still be aggressively treated. With hospice, treatment shifts from aggressively pursuing a cure to keeping the patient comfortable and giving them a quality of life for whatever time they have remaining. This care can be provided at home, in a hospital, in a nursing home, or in an inpatient hospice program. Unfortunately, Jill did not feel that she had an adequate understanding of the options, until it was too late.

In a matter of one day, I had three similar conversations with other families. I quickly realized that this was what our healthcare team in the ICU dealt with every single day. This experience was the norm, not the exception. Jill and Gary's experience was just one of hundreds and hundreds of patients and families that I have worked with since that time, who grappled with end-of-life decision-making. Countless families face these very situations every single day.

Throughout my time in the ICU, I had similar, almost daily conversations with loved ones of patients who were critically-ill or dying. Some patients recovered and others did not. It was my role to help the families through that process. Mine was a role of profound importance, and one that I was honored to have. I had countless experiences with patients and their loved ones who faced end-of-life issues and decisions. I saw it as an honor to be with people as they made their transition and also a massive responsibility. Life and death are as real and raw an experience as it gets.

I also became very aware of the role that my work played with patients and their loved ones and how they experienced death, particularly for those who were left to deal with the memory of that experience for the rest of their lives. The decisions that they made, the space that was held for them, how their loved one's transition took place, how they were allowed to grieve; all of these things forever shaped that memory for them.

I realized that I could have a significant impact on how they experienced the loss of their loved one, by simply holding space for them to be present, to acknowledge their grief, to reassure them that there was no manual on how to do this "right." By helping them to speak as their loved one's voice, rather than from their own wishes. By honoring the pivotal moment that this experience would be in their lives. By helping them navigate and understand the process. By just being with them, patiently, lovingly, without judgment. Wherever they were.

Jill has shared many times that working with me through the loss of her husband transformed how she was able to process the experience, and allowed her to release the guilt and second-guessing about the decisions made leading up to his passing. I realized that it was a unique and profoundly special skill to have, as a "transformational space-holder," as I came to describe my role.

Becoming a Teacher

There were a number of opportunities in the hospital, as a teaching facility, for me to continue to explore working with end-of-life issues. I served on the committee that helped form the curriculum for physicians and other healthcare providers to facilitate conversations at the end of life. In my role in the ICU, I had the opportunity to work with the interns and residents, who, newly out of med school, often had limited experience in having these conversations with patients and their loved ones. I was able to teach them how to allow people to explore their wishes around their own death, to allow families to discuss what their loved one may have wanted if they did not leave their wishes in an advance directive or living will, and to facilitate conversations exploring the concept of what 'quality of life' meant.

I continued to work in end-of-life care over several years, in oncology, palliative care, hospice, and long-term care. What I realized during that time, is that it is a gift to be able to speak comfortably with patients, their families, and loved ones about the experience of death and dying. It takes a person with a particular view of life to be able to speak about death and dying as a spiritual experience. Not just as a physical experience, but as a deeply spiritual and transformational experience for those who are dying, as well as for those who are left to process the death of a loved one; those who are left behind.

It became a mission for me to educate doctors and other healthcare providers about how to explore life, death, and dying with patients and their families. In doing so, I realized that I had an ability to speak with people about this subject that many found to be difficult and uncomfortable to discuss. I had a number of experiences that I realized were incredibly profound and life-defining. I was present when many, many patients made their transition from this physical world. I had reverence for the process, and saw it as an incredible honor and gift to be with someone at such an authentic, intimate moment.

I began a journey, unknown to me at that time, to explore, on a very deep level, what life and death mean. What conscious living and conscious dying mean. What awakening to your life's journey and your soul's purpose means. What living your legacy and leaving your legacy mean.

A Shared Passion

My mother was a nurse who worked for many years in geriatrics. We had a deep connection around our devotion to end-of-life work and being available to patients and families at the time of their transition. We had a passion and a great respect for the spiritual experience that can happen for those who are dying and their loved ones at the end of life. We also shared a deep regard for the importance of living wills and advance directives. I loved working with end-of-life issues and with those who were dying, and I knew that I had a gift for it. In fact, when I left that work after giving birth to my daughter, I always said that I would come back to it at some point. I didn't know how returning to the work would look, but I was sure that it would come full circle one day.

Because we had this shared connection, my mom and I had the opportunity over many years to share and discuss experiences that we had in both our personal and professional lives, as well as to share our own values, beliefs, and choices about the end of our lives. This was a special connection that I felt privileged and honored to share with my mom. I didn't realize at the time what an invaluable gift that it was, nor did I know that this deep connection that we shared around the importance of advance directives would later come to play a pivotal role in both of our lives.

My mother and I had many talks over the years that were on a deeply spiritual level, about life, death, and dying. We both also had our own personal experiences. In addition to the loss of my father when I was just 15 years old, I also lost both of my grandmothers to breast cancer when I was in my later 20's; and my paternal grandfather to complications from dementia. My maternal grandfather was the last of my grandparents to die, living to 100 years old, staying in his home of nearly 70 years until the time of his death.

A "Good Death"

Both of my grandmothers died in their early 70's from breast cancer. They, like my maternal grandfather, were on hospice care, and were at home until their deaths. Both were surrounded by family and died peacefully and comfortably. When my dad's mom died, I was 28, and had just had back surgery following a car accident injury. I was still in a lot of pain and I remember being at my grandparents' home along with many other family members, as it was clear that my grandmother was near the end of her life. We have a large family, so there were many family members in and out of the bedroom. At one point, I crawled into my grandmother's bed and lay next to her, just to be close to her.

Her breathing was so shallow and slowed, that there were several times when we actually thought she had passed. But then she would take another breath. Then, as clear as day, she opened her eyes and sort of lifted her head and said, "It's time for me to go now. Vern's here and he's telling me it's time to go with him". She looked straight ahead as though she were looking right at my dad, Vern. She passed that night.

I believe that my dad was there, and that she was between worlds at that time and saw him. It gave me tremendous comfort to know that he was there to greet her and help her to cross over. I've seen it happen countless times, when one is near transitioning and they see someone that has already passed, right there in the room with them, to guide them as they make their transition.

Both of my grandmothers as well as my maternal grandfather, experienced peaceful deaths at home, in spite of their illnesses and age. They were kept comfortable with the support of hospice care and surrounded by their loved ones. Just as I have seen countless times over the years, personally and professionally, both of my grandmothers had one child that had to travel from a farther distance, and both waited for that last child to arrive before they let go. They needed to know that everyone was there. They needed to know that everyone would be okay. They needed permission to let go.

It was important to each of them that they remain in the comfort of their own homes until their deaths. They wanted to have their pain well-controlled, and be with their loved ones in familiar, peaceful surroundings. Indeed, their wishes were honored. They were enveloped in love, compassion, care, and support, surrounded by their large families. They were kept comfortable, without compromising their ability to enjoy meaningful time with their loved ones, right up until their deaths, thanks to the loving, supportive care of hospice.

That is what I call a "good death."

PART II

A WAKE-UP CALL

That Day

On a hot July morning in 2014, my husband received a phone call that would change our lives forever. Because I was the only one of five children in my family living out-of-state, literally across the country, my brother called my husband to make sure that he was with me when they shared the news. My husband pulled into the driveway as I sat on the front steps with my then-four-year-old daughter. He got out of the car and told me to call my brother immediately. I knew from the look on his face that something was terribly wrong. "It's your mom," he said.

When I get my brother on the phone, I learn that my mom has taken a horrific fall down her basement stairs onto the concrete floor. She suffered massive head trauma, and is bleeding from her ears and nose. She is unconscious, but alive. She is taken by life-flight to the nearest trauma center. My brother, his voice cracking, tells me that it doesn't look good.

I know from my years of experience as a social worker in intensive care and emergency departments that blood coming from the ears and nose is a grave sign. I am also aware that the chances of her surviving this injury are very, very poor. My immediate thought is about what my mother's wishes are for the end of her life.

We had talked about her desires countless times. She felt strongly that, in the absence of a spouse to make decisions on her behalf, that her eldest child, my brother, should be her primary health care power of attorney (the person appointed in an advance directive to make health care decisions on one's behalf). But she also knew that it might be difficult for him to make decisions involving withdrawal of care if she were ever in a situation in which there was little chance for meaningful recovery.

I completely respected her wish to have my brother serve as her primary health care power of attorney. I also knew that I would feel very comfortable with making any decisions that needed to be made on her behalf, simply because of the work that I had done for many years, the countless conversations that I had with her, and the comfort that I had with end-of-life issues. She knew that I would ensure, even in the most difficult or ambiguous of circumstances, that her wishes were honored, no matter how difficult. She knew that I could and would do that, so she agreed to appoint me as secondary Power of Attorney after my brother.

My mom's youngest sister, who is also a nurse, meets the life-flight helicopter as soon as it lands and talks to the neurosurgeons at the trauma center. The plan is to immediately take her to surgery. I talk briefly with my aunt by phone and ask her to tell my mom to hang in there until I get there. By the time I travel across the country and arrive at the hospital, it is a full 12 hours after receiving the initial call. It is the longest 12 hours of my entire life.

Following emergency neurosurgery, we learn that my mom suffered massive skull fractures in both the front and back of her head. The surgeons are able to remove a large blood clot just under the front of her skull; however, during surgery it also becomes apparent that there are several other bleeds on her brain.

I spend the entire night on a cot next to my mom, alone with her in her hospital room. I rub her hands, moisten her lips, clean her face, talk to her, sing to her, put videos of my children up next to her ear so that she can hear them. I just need to be there with her. I need to take care of her. I need her to know how grateful I am that she waited for me to get there. I know that this is a life-changing moment and that the decisions that lay ahead for my siblings and me will forever impact us. I realize that this is quite possibly the last night that I will have with my mom.

The following day, my siblings and I have some very difficult conversations ahead of us as we meet with the entire care team, including doctors, surgeons, pastoral care, and the palliative care team. What they tell us, essentially, is that the neurological damage is profound. The extent of damage to my mom's brain is simply incompatible with any meaningful recovery. They share with us that, if she survives, there is a great likelihood that she will be in a permanent vegetative state (a coma).

The team also shares that they have never before seen an advance directive like my mother's. She has made her wishes for the end of her life quite clear, even in these one-in-a-million, ambiguous circumstances. We know instinctively that our mother would never want to live in a permanent vegetative state. However, there is always that miracle chance that if they do another surgery, it may possibly open a window of opportunity, though we know that is very, very small likelihood.

My siblings and I gather around a table in the hospital conference room to read her advance directive together. As I read it aloud, it is almost as though she is there in that room speaking directly to us. She is very clear in terms of her wishes for her care, to not be kept alive or sustained on artificial support and to not have heroic measures taken if there is little chance for meaningful recovery or quality of life.

It is as though she has prepared her advance directive knowing that the one-in-a-million odds of her experiencing what she did, was exactly what would ultimately lead to her death. Every question that we have is answered. Not only that, but she also has handwritten messages directly to us, things that are important to her that we carry with us and live by. Things like, "Always keep family traditions," "Stay together," "Never let anything come between you," "Know that you were made from love," and "Forgive one another."

True to form, my mom also writes that she will leave the details of her services up to us kids, yet at the same time, provides nearly every detail of her service and arrangements. She makes it clear that she wants to be cremated, where she wants her ashes spread, who she wants us to be sure to include in her service, and what specific songs she wants played. She even lets us know which funeral director she wants and provides his personal cell phone number ("But I'll leave the details up to all of you..."). It not only gives us a good laugh at one of the most difficult times of our lives because it is so "classic Mom," but her directive also makes us feel as though she is right there with us, speaking directly to us, knowing that we need that light-hearted moment.

*My mom gives us the gift of being at peace with the incredibly difficult decision to remove her from life support, because we know, beyond a shadow of a doubt, that it is **her** decision. We know that we are simply carrying out her wishes. Not only has she lifted that burden, it feels like we are able to give her the gift of having her voice heard and her wishes honored. We know that it is a gift to her to know that her children will not be left feeling guilty or carrying a burden about her death.*

You Are My Sunshine

When we were young, my family used to take road trips in the car and sing old hymns and folk songs like "Found a Peanut," "Do Lord," and "You Are My Sunshine." My mom, my younger sister Cate, and I had our own special version of these sing-alongs that we called "Counselor Catie's Campfire Choir."

My mom is removed from life support and placed on comfort measures (a medical term basically meaning that the only interventions are to keep one comfortable until they die), the tubes and machines are removed and she is cleaned up. She looks like our mom again, like she is resting peacefully. We sit around her bed, holding hands, singing her favorite songs from our road-trip days. We pray, cry, laugh, and share memories together. It is the most beautiful, powerful experience of simply connecting with her and with each other.

We joke about how she snored really loudly when she was over-tired, and how we would give anything to hear her snore just one more time. As though hearing our conversation, when the tube is removed and she is peaceful and comfortable, my mom starts snoring, and it is the most beautiful, soothing sound I've ever heard.

I feel her presence in the room with us at that moment, like she is no longer struggling, but is just at peace, as we are simply allowed to BE with her, peacefully and vulnerably, until she is ready to let go. We each talk to her, give her permission to let go, and let her know that we and the grandkids will be okay. We tell her that we love her and will see her again. She appears comfortable and peaceful, as her breathing slowly becomes more shallow. As I exit the room to get my brothers, leaving my sister alone with my mom, she takes her last breath. It is a perfect honoring of my sister to be alone with her at that moment because they have a very special bond. As my brothers and I walk back in the room, my sister quietly says, "She's gone." It is profoundly painful, but it is lovely and peaceful and beautiful, all at the same time.

My mother's last love letter to her children and her grandchildren was in the form of her advance directive that clearly told us what was important to her and what she wanted. That directive lifted a weight from our shoulders of having to question whether we would make the right decisions. It was as though she knew exactly what we needed to hear to be able to let her go. Reading it in her own handwriting was even more special; we were able to read her own words as though she was speaking directly to us.

Dark Night of the Soul

The days that followed my mother's passing were a blur. I stayed in Wisconsin with my family for about ten days. I was constantly surrounded by loved ones. I was either with my siblings, reading through cards, going through my mom's belongings, or with my large network of extended family. For those ten days, the grief was manageable; there was a lot of support and many tasks to keep me distracted.

Once I returned back home to Texas, though, and was no longer surrounded by family, the grief hit me. Hard. It was overwhelming. As I had with my dad's death, I felt like I was just sucker-punched, and the grief knocked the wind right out of me. I was not prepared for the crash; I really thought that I was handling things, that I was doing a pretty good job of coping with my grief. The reality though, is that I did a really good job of compartmentalizing and shutting off those parts of me that felt the pain, so that I could continue to function in my daily life.

Work had always been the space in which I could continue to be effective, regardless of what was going on with my personal life. I continued to see clients and work well with them. Outside of that, though, there was little semblance of normalcy, or of healthy functioning. At the most random of times, something would trigger my grief, seemingly out of nowhere, and it would render me utterly paralyzed.

About a week after returning to my home in Texas from Wisconsin, I sat on my back patio, talking on the phone to a friend of mine. For the first time since my mom's accident, I walked through the events that I had experienced over those nearly two weeks and the intense roller coaster of emotions. I talked about that first phone call with my brother, the 12 hours of traveling to get to the hospital, seeing my mom for the first time, spending the night holding her hand and talking to her, holding the phone to her ear playing videos of my girls.

I told my friend about my mom's advance directive and how profound a gift it was to me and my siblings. I shared how I held the phone to my mom's ear so that my husband and godmother could say goodbye to her before she let go. I talked about the funeral, writing and delivering the eulogy, and the hundreds of people at her service. With intensifying emotion and that sock-in-the-gut feeling, I described going to her apartment for the first time, seeing where she fell, and curling up in the fetal position, sobbing, in that exact spot on the basement floor, with evidence of the fall still visible in the broken handrail on the concrete floor.

Up until that point, I was so busy with making decisions, planning my mom's services, writing her eulogy, and going through her belongings, I hadn't had time to think about everything that happened and everything that we all went through. Before I realized what was happening, I was sobbing and crying so loudly that I thought surely the entire block could hear me. That deep, wrenching, guttural kind of sob that you can't control even if you wanted to.

The pain was so deep, it was indescribable. My friend listened to me, cried with me, just let me lose complete control, and kept telling me that I was okay. For that whole two weeks after Mom's passing, I felt like if I allowed myself to feel the emotion at all, if I turned that faucet on even just a little, it would flood the whole damn place and I would surely drown in it along with everyone else around me. That night, sitting there on my back patio, I turned on the faucet. And I felt it. Deep. Horribly, painfully deep.

When I finally came back to the present moment and was able to stop the agonized sobbing and get my breath back, I realized just how deep my grief was. It frightened me, yet I realized that allowing myself to finally feel the pain of my grief wasn't nearly as terrifying as what I made up in my mind about feeling it. The FEAR of feeling the pain of my grief was what kept me paralyzed more than the pain of the grief itself.

I also became aware of something else that night. As I shared the entire experience with my friend, she was in awe of my mother's advance directive and how powerful a role it played in her transition and my experience. At that moment, it dawned on me. THIS is it. This is the full circle that I knew I would someday come back to in my work with death and dying.

I needed to educate people about the power of advance directives and conversations about end-of-life care, about the impact that they can have on families and their experience concerning their loved one's death. I needed to share how, even in the most painful and confusing of circumstances, that document could be the gift that has the power to forever change people's memories of their loved one's passing. This is what my mom and I had talked about so many times over all those years – the importance and the gift of having an advance directive. This is what she felt passionately about. I realized in that moment that this calling was what I was meant to do and that it would also be my gift to my mom - to carry on her legacy.

Coming Clean

I knew at that moment that I had a calling on my life that I needed to answer. That deep connection, that raw, vulnerable authenticity, that touch with the divine that I experienced in my work in oncology, hospice, and end-of-life care. I needed to teach about the importance of preparing advance directives and to elevate a dignified, candid, life-affirming conversation around death and dying. I needed to teach people about embracing life NOW and living their legacy, because tomorrow isn't promised.

This was the full circle that my life's work would bring me to and I knew it in my gut, in my soul; yet, I was so deep in my grief at that time that I couldn't act on that calling. Instead, I drowned my grief, sadness, anger, and fear in alcohol for a year and a half following my mom's death.

It was a terribly dark time. I could hardly teach others about living life authentically and powerfully when I was essentially living a lie, in fear, isolation, and emptiness. The grief over the loss of my mom was like a punch in the gut, though I didn't realize the depth of the sadness that I experienced. What I didn't fully appreciate at the time was how each loss that we experience causes the unresolved grief from previous losses to resurface. I wasn't prepared for the compounding effect that the loss of my mom, along with all of my previous losses, would have on me emotionally. It felt like one loss, disappointment, or hurt after another, that just built up this wall of darkness.

So, I hid out from the world.

On the exterior, I could hold things together pretty well. From the time I was a kid growing up in a chaotic and unstable home, I had become adept at compartmentalizing my life so that I could still function in certain areas, even while life was a shit show in other areas. When it came to my work, I was still a damn good therapist and coach. Even during the times that my life was complete dysfunctional chaos, somehow I was always able to help people create powerful shifts in their lives. I just had a gift for it. I was able to show up authentically and powerfully for others, wearing my humanness on my sleeve and walking in my own imperfection, which allowed me to connect easily with the people I worked with.

I've always been vulnerable and authentic with my clients, but clearly, I could not fully be my authentic self when I went home every day and drowned my pain in a bottle of wine. Work was good for me, though; at least it offered a diversion for a while. I had always been taught that the best way to get out of your own garbage is to focus outwardly and help someone else. That, I could do.

I also had a young daughter at home that I needed to be present for. It's hard to be depressed when you have a goofy, energetic, full-of-life five-year old reminding you every day about what is really important in life. Still, every night, after I saw my clients and did my 'adulting' duties, I shut myself off from the world, including my husband and friends, to be back in my pain and darkness. I literally closed the door on the world. I stayed in my room, alone, wine glass in hand. It was hard to sleep at night, and even harder to wake up and face the next day. I felt completely alone, lonely, and lost. I had no idea how or if I would ever get beyond that feeling. The pain just got deeper and deeper. The deeper the pain got, the more I tried to numb it.

On the last night of that year-and-a-half-long binge, after a tense disagreement with my husband, I had my usual glass of wine in hand (likely the third or fourth of the night if I'm being honest). As we walked out to the back patio to continue our discussion, I literally tripped over my own two feet. I went head first over the patio table, my elbows hit the ground and one leg flew up in the air. But I'll be damned if I was about to let that glass of wine go; I didn't spill a bit. I tried to keep myself from fully face-planting, yelling at my husband to help me, but when he offered his hand, I yelled, "No, grab my drink before it spills!"

I got up and dusted myself off, feeling a bit embarrassed about my near face-plant and when I looked up, I caught my husband's eye. The look on his face stopped me cold. It was a cross between pity and disgust, as though to say, "Seriously? You're literally falling over drunk and you're worried about your f'n drink?" The sad truth was, that's exactly what I was most worried about at that moment.

I woke up the following morning, embarrassed about the night before and too hung over to help get my kindergartner off to school. Yet there I was, feeling like shit but still trying to figure out how I could get a drink without my husband knowing, just so I could get rid of the shakes and nausea.

What in the hell am I DOING?, I thought out loud as I stared at myself in the mirror, looking years older than my age, dark circles under my eyes, my skin a dry, pale gray. I started thinking about how many years of therapy my kids would need because I had screwed up their lives. That trusty old mom-guilt washed right over me like a freaking tsunami.

This is complete and utter BULLSHIT. Enough is enough.

The grief over the loss of my mom was raw and I just wasn't able to find my way out of the pain or the drinking. I came to realize that if I knew how to heal it on my own, I would have already done it. I wouldn't have remained in that pit of despair for 18 months. I was busted all to bupkus and it was clear that I didn't know how to get through the grief on my own. So, I asked for help.

I asked for help in such a way that I had to share the secret that I kept from most people (except for my husband, though I kept the degree of it even from him). I acknowledged my problem. I owned it. I accepted that I simply couldn't heal this pain alone. I cleaned out all of the empty bottles of wine that I had hidden in my closet and various spots around the house, many that I had completely forgotten about. I got rid of the rest of the alcohol that was left and I got the help that I needed.

I found an amazing doctor who was a soft-spoken, gentle yet direct, highly-skilled physician who specialized in treating addictions. As soon as I left his office after that first visit, I knew that I had just taken the first step toward my healing, and that it was time to own it. I realized that this path was what I needed to do in order to move forward with what I had come to believe was my life's work. I did what my doctor suggested. I quit drinking, quit smoking pot, and quit eating to numb myself, along with the help of medication, until the neurons in my brain started firing in the right way again. I surrounded myself with people who were growing and evolving in their own lives. I dove into personal-development work and participated in transformational workshops and coaching.

When I finally began to emerge from the fog of despair and near-drowning in alcohol, there was a clarity that came to me. I had been emotionally dead for a year and a half. I needed to breathe myself back to life before I could support others in living their best lives. So, I dug in and I did the work of clearing out the mental and emotional garbage that held me back. I faced the grief head-on. I released the worry, doubt, fear, lack, and limitation that I carried. Figuratively and literally, I released that weight - 45 pounds of mental, emotional, physical, and spiritual weight.

I stopped hiding out and started living again. I healed and renewed my relationships, began enjoying and participating in life again, and, most importantly, I started to dream again. Except this time, I knew my dreams were not only possible, but were totally, absolutely achievable. Once that fog of 18 months of near-daily drinking began to lift, I slowly emerged. I went from being emotionally curled up in the fetal position to crawling. Slowly, as I experienced sobriety for the first time since my mom's death, I began to stand upright, and then walk on my own.

The Clearing

Though it took some time to get to that healing, eventually I did. I had to dig deep. I had to excavate my own life, those dark parts of me that I was ashamed of and didn't want anyone else to see. Those deeply-rooted fears, doubts, and worries. The beliefs of lack and limitation that I held for many, many years. The things about my past that I thought that I had released and cleared that still needed more healing. I grieved the losses I experienced in my life. I received personal coaching. I reconnected with my spiritual practices. I began to gain control of emotions that I had felt unable to manage for many years, particularly resentment, anger, fear, guilt, and shame.

I devoured personal development and leadership work. I participated in, staffed, coached, and facilitated healing, transformational workshops, and leadership programs. I worked on healing the relationships in my own life that needed healing. I learned to recognize the habits, beliefs, and patterns of self-sabotage that held me back for so long. I built relationships with people that were willing to grow with me and hold me accountable. I let go of those relationships that no longer served me or the other person. I built my tribe.

I took responsibility. It was messy at times, it hurt, it was painful, and sometimes even ugly. The journey was by no means a straight line. It was often a two-steps-forward, five-steps-back sort of pattern, yet I stayed committed. Eventually, those two steps forward turned into six, and the five steps back turned into one or two, and I became really okay with that cycle.

I realized that life IS this constant spiral, and, if we take responsibility, do the work, remain patient and persistent, and stick with it, we move in a constant <u>upward</u> spiral.

The curve balls, the hardships, setbacks, losses, and pain, are all NATURAL. They are NORMAL. Just as natural and normal as the joys, successes, breakthroughs, and triumphs in our journey. They are of equal importance and I firmly believe that it is precisely those moments "in the valley" that are our biggest opportunities for growth and breakthrough.

I learned to expect the unexpected, and to know that all was still well. I accepted that I have a biological predisposition toward depression, addiction, and anxiety. I began to understand that there may continue to be periods in my life when that biology rears its head, and that it is absolutely okay to go back to my support system, work with a coach, or return to my doctor and go back on medications for a period of time, if that support is what is needed.

I began to accept those parts of me that weren't so pretty or were downright ugly. The history of my life led to some of my negative thought patterns, and the habits and behaviors were not healthy or supportive of the direction

I wanted to head in my life. Once I accepted those realities, truly, lovingly, completely, and without judgment, my emotional crawl turned into a walk, then turned into a jog, that turned into a run, that started to take flight... and I began to soar. I began to get clear about the direction that my life and my life's work were headed.

PART III

3 KEYS TO LIVING WITH JOY, PEACE, AND PURPOSE

What Truly Matters in the End

I knew that I wanted to help others get beyond their fears about death, to start having conversations about how they wanted to LIVE **and** how they wanted to leave this physical world. I wanted to help them make their wishes known and complete their advance directives so that, like my family, their loved ones could take even a tragic, traumatic loss and make it a beautiful, healing experience.

More than that, I wanted to help people to:

- live in the NOW - authentically and openly

- be joyful, abundant, and grateful

- live each day as though it could be their last

- go for their dreams and no longer WAIT until…

- enable the dreams of others

- get excited about life and make memories with those that matter most

- get clear about what is important to them and what legacy they want to leave

- stay in ACTION to **live** that legacy every day

Because today is all we have.

I wanted to support people as they asked and answered the questions, "Who am I, really? What TRULY matters to me? What do I DESERVE? Why am I NECESSARY?" I wanted to help people to feel confident that, when they depart this life, that they would do so having played full-out, leaving a powerful legacy, and giving their loved ones the gifts of peace, clarity, and healing so that they could look back with no regrets.

One of the many things that I learned during my years of working with the dying, was that those who are dying do often want to talk about the fact that they are dying. Many times, they don't openly discuss it, not because of their own discomfort, but because of their loved ones' discomfort. Often, the person who is dying has come to terms with their impending death even though their loved ones have not. Their loved ones may feel as though, if they don't talk about it, then maybe death won't actually happen. **If only they were that powerful.**

Through those many conversations, I learned that when we get to the end of our lives, what is important to us is very simple. Our focus is all about the relationships in our lives and our fulfilled or unfulfilled dreams. That's it. The "stuff" that we acquired, the "success" we thought we either achieved or didn't achieve, what kind of house we owned, what car we drove, the job we had, how big or small our bank accounts were; none of that matters.

What people focus on at the end of life is their relationships, their dreams, and their sense of fulfillment. We don't wish for more material "stuff." **We want to know that we matter.** We wish for living life more and having better relationships.

Patients who were dying said things to me like, "I wish I had been a better father." "I wish I had spent more time with my kids when they were growing up." "I wish that I had traveled more and experienced more of the world." "I wish that I told my parents that I loved and appreciated them more." "I wish that I had taken more risks and gone for my dreams."

Most of all, they wished that they had spent less time hanging onto resentments and old hurts, and more time forgiving, healing, and loving. THAT is what matters most at the end of our lives. The lessons I learned from those conversations were immensely life-changing.

I realized that, in order for people to live life with **no regrets**, they needed to have the tools to live their best life **today**. To be present and happy; free of worry, doubt, and fear. To forgive what they needed to forgive and ask for forgiveness that they needed to ask for. To say what they needed to say. To let go of the past. To love deeply. To risk. To live their dreams. To be who they were truly meant to be. To be the best version of themselves. To live authentically, consciously, and abundantly. To do their work. To be okay with who they are and how they have lived their lives, mistakes, flaws, and all. My mission and my vision became for my own life and experience to be a vessel, a catalyst for others to be at peace, live fully, and look back on their lives with total freedom.

In addition to the gift of her advance directive, what gave me peace in my mom's passing was knowing that, in the last several years of her life, she made a decision to start living life for HER. Like so many women in midlife, she had spent far too much of her life doing what she thought others needed, wanted, or expected of her. But she made a decision to let go of the fear of judgment and the need to please others. She made a CHOICE to do what brought her peace and fulfillment. As a result, for several years prior to her death, she spent countless weekends at a cabin on a lake, fishing off of a pontoon boat with her good friend and furry four-legged companion. It brought me such peace knowing that she spent those last years of her life doing what brought her joy - BEFORE it was too late.

Her decision to focus on her own peace and happiness is what inspired me to create my transformational coaching programs for other powerful, deserving women in midlife, who, like my mom, have spent far too much of their lives putting others first, while putting their own dreams and desires on the back burner. I do my speaking, coaching, and writing so that I can share the gifts that have come from my own journey, because I know that we have ALL had experiences like mine that served as a wake-up call in our lives. I created my programs so that, like my mom, others can also experience the fulfilled life **they** deserve - **BEFORE it's too late.**

The sections that follow are the tenets that my work is based on. The three keys presented are adapted from the tenets that I teach in my transformational coaching programs and workshops.

1. Evolution

2. Contribution

3. Live each day JOYfully

The purpose of these keys is to help you create a life that you are totally JAZZED about and ENJOY it with those that matter most...**while** making an impact on the planet.

You can learn more about my programs and working with me at http://deanne-joy.com/work-with-me/.

Key #1: Evolution

These are the exact tools, techniques, and mindset strategies that I applied to my own life when I was a young adult trying to start a career as a therapist but still struggling on the journey of healing my own wounds. I used them during difficult times in my marriage and years into my career when I was a burned-out therapist, having spent years giving and giving from an empty cup, feeling that I wasn't living **fully**, or living my TRUE purpose. They are also the same methods that I applied to my life as I was healing from the grief of losing my mom.

These keys are simple actions and strategies that you can do every day to move you toward a more grounded, confident, and joyful version of you. Remember, your job is to live a fulfilled and joyful life so that whenever the time comes for you to leave this physical planet, you can look back on your life with **no regrets**, knowing that you played full-out, went for your dreams, and enjoyed life with those that matter most - while leaving an impact that **makes a difference.**

You can accomplish this by asking yourself the same question that we started with: *"If today were my last day on this physical earth, would I be happy with how I lived my life?"* Rather than fearing or avoiding the reality of your finite life, use it as your gauge for how you are living life TODAY.

100% Responsibility

OWN the choices you make in your life. Be willing to look at how you got to where you are, choice by choice by choice. Responsibility does not mean blame. It simply means that you own ALL of your choices and ALL of the results in your life. Not from a place of judgment; just simply own all of them - good, bad, ugly, or indifferent.

Call out the things that do not work for you and take steps to change them. Look at the old beliefs, habits, and patterns that no longer work for you or hold you back from creating the life you truly want and deserve. Most of these patterns are not even in our conscious awareness; they are often simply carried over from experiences earlier in life. We end up carrying those old wounds and repeating the same dysfunctional patterns. Work to bring them to your awareness, call them out, and then take responsibility for changing them.

If you continue to engage in beliefs, habits, or patterns that do not work for you EVEN after recognizing them, be willing to take a look at what the payoff is for keeping them. Maybe holding on to them allows you to escape responsibility, avoid dealing with painful emotions or circumstances, or make excuses to continue to play small and not create the life you truly want and deserve. It's ok if it is. It's not about judging, just noticing and acknowledging.

Once you name a thing and call it what it is, you immediately disempower it. Recognize what no longer works for you and acknowledge it by journaling or by speaking it out loud to someone you trust. You'll be amazed at how quickly it loses its power and begins to shift. What is one old belief, habit, or pattern that is not working for you? Think of one right now. Be honest and own it. And then celebrate that shit, because that is a huge win; once you acknowledge what needs to be changed, you can actually do the work to **change it.**

What I know now is that every single event, experience, and relationship that I have had in my life has led me to right where I am today. My life today is the aggregate of ALL of these experiences. Without any single one of them, I would not be who or where I am in my life now. Making this connection allows me to be grateful for those experiences rather than seeing myself as damaged goods for having experienced them.

We are MORE than the worst things we have ever done, or the worst things that have happened to us. In order for us to experience a life of peace and joy, we must take 100% responsibility for our life and our outcomes. While we are not necessarily responsible for the things that happen "to" us, we ARE responsible for how we choose to **respond** to those experiences **today**. Find the "blessons" (blessings + lessons) in every experience, especially those that feel really shitty at the time; those are the **greatest** opportunities for growth.

You are not the result of the things that have happened to you. You are not a product of your past. You can choose the lens through which you see your life. You can **choose** suffering, or you can turn your pain into purpose. You can **choose** to be in your power, rather than a victim of your circumstances. You can **choose** to see every situation as an opportunity for you to learn, grow, and evolve (yes, even the shitty ones). You can **choose** to see life as happening "for" you rather than "to" you.

Being responsible isn't easy. It's certainly not always pretty. Being responsible means that we must humble ourselves and really, truly, no-shit, be willing to take a hard look at our choices and behaviors. The power that is in that responsibility is ENORMOUS, because it means that you have CHOICE.

Own who you are, the choices you make in your life, and your outcomes, without judging them as right, wrong, good, or bad. They just ARE. And you have the power to change them.

The question is, **will you be bold enough to make that choice and accept that challenge?**

Your Thoughts Create Your Reality

Understand that **you are NOT your thoughts.** Your thoughts are just that - thoughts. They don't control you; you control them. The thoughts in your mind did not come from outside of you. They came from YOU! **You create the thoughts in your mind, and you have the power to change them.**

Think for just a moment about a time in your life when you felt sad. Don't dwell on the moment too much, just enough to remember and know what it felt like. How did you feel when you thought of that event? Sad, right? How long did it take you to get there? Seconds, probably. What did you have to do to feel that way? All you had to do was **think** about a time that you felt that way before.

Now, think of a time in your life when you felt JOYFUL. Step into that moment as though you are there right now, seeing it through your own eyes, hearing the sounds around you, and **feeling the feelings of joy right now**. How did you feel when you remembered that time? You felt joyful, right? How long did it take you to go from feeling sad to joyful? Seconds, right? And what did you have to do to get there? Again, all you did was **think about a time when you felt that way.**

In a matter of moments, you changed how you felt **just by** thinking about past experiences where you felt the way you WANT to feel. You see, you are not your mind. Your thoughts create your emotions, not the other way around. You don't feel sad and **then** think of something sad. You feel sad **because** you are thinking of something sad.

Always focus on what you WANT, not what you don't want. When you focus on what you don't want ("I don't want to be broke," "I don't want to be lonely," "I don't want to be depressed."), you attract that same vibration to you, which means you end up getting the very thing that you said that you don't want.

To your unconscious mind, your thoughts <u>are</u> reality. It doesn't know the difference between what you think or imagine, and what you actually experience. Therefore, the thoughts that you think in your mind create your reality. Let that just sink in for a moment! **Your thoughts become your reality.**

If you want to understand why you create the results you have in your life, simply look at the conversations you have in your mind. Working with someone who can help reveal those blind spots can be really useful. We can't see what we can't see. Be willing to invest in yourself. Do the work. Get a coach, an accountability partner, a spiritual counselor, or a therapist. Find someone who can help you see the subconscious thoughts and patterns that you aren't yet able to see on your own.

Our God-given Healing Gifts

Two of the most POWERFUL healing tools available on earth are innate gifts that we are all born with. They are the God-given gifts of breath and imagination. When we tap into the power of these two profound gifts, change can happen quickly and easily.

I've worked with thousands of people over the past 25 years. I've worked with women in their 50s, 60s, and even 70s who still carried baggage from their childhood with them, not even aware that it was spilling over into their relationships, parenting, careers, and how they saw themselves.

They were AMAZED at how quickly and easily we could actually shift those old programs and patterns to create massive transformation in our lives and relationships. Especially when we tap into our God-given healing gifts of breath and imagination, have the proper support and guidance, and learn effective tools to help us along the way.

So often, we make things much more difficult than they need to be. When you keep it simple and use the tools and gifts that you already have, you will start to see shifts happen much more quickly and easily.

You are MORE than Enough

We all have some feeling of, "I'm not smart enough, not educated enough, not pretty enough, not skinny enough, not rich enough...." Ultimately, all of those "I'm not _____ enough" conversations come down to, simply, "I'm not enough." I am not worthy or capable because I am not enough. We've all had some version of this negative self-talk at some point in our lives; it's part of the human condition.

I've worked with folks who are homeless or on drugs, young moms on welfare, people with mental illness, working moms, actors, musicians, directors, business owners, and corporate CEOs. I've worked with people who have no money and some with more money than God. What I know is, the "I'm not enoughness" does not discriminate. It doesn't matter what you have, what you've accomplished, what size home you live in, or what your zip code is. Every single person that I have ever worked with or encountered has had those thoughts and beliefs of not being enough on some level at some point in their lives.

It's really important for you to understand that those thoughts and beliefs are a result of some earlier experience in your life that you need to gain resolution on, or someone else's opinion of you. What I know for sure, is that those "not enough" thoughts and beliefs are ALL lies. The magnificence and brilliance of the human body, mind, and spirit and the miracle of your existence inherently counter the notion that you are not enough. Do you realize that scientists estimate that the chances of becoming a human being are 400 TRILLION TO ONE??? So, yep, you're pretty much a freaking miracle. You are enough because you are HERE. You are enough because you were BORN. You are **enough**.

When we love, accept, and forgive ourselves, embracing our perfect imperfections, we discover where true joy comes from. Let go of the need to be perfect. Perfectionism is simply another form of believing, "I'm not enough." It is self-judgment. When we have a need to be perfect, we constantly second-guess ourselves.

Perfection is the opposite of excellence. When we hold ourselves to an unrealistic standard, we unconsciously believe that, "If the world only knew; if they saw who I truly was, they would know that I am a fraud. They would know that I don't have it all together. They would know that I don't measure up." Ultimately, "They would know that I am not enough."

There is nothing about you that is broken. There is nothing about you that needs to be fixed. You are perfectly imperfect, in all your humanness, with all of your flaws, with all of the dark parts of you that you desperately try to keep hidden. What allows others to truly connect with us on a deeper level is our willingness to be vulnerable and authentic. When we are simply our human, deeply-flawed selves, it gives others permission to be human and deeply flawed as well.

Teach People How to Treat You

We teach people how to treat us. The world looks to you as the example of how you should be treated, and it will follow your lead. You cannot expect the world to treat you with kindness, compassion, and unconditional love if you aren't willing to give them to yourself. When you truly love and accept yourself, it allows you to get beyond the bullshit stories you tell yourself that keep holding you back so that you can get in touch with your life's purpose, the reason that you are here; to share the gifts you were put here to share.

There is simply no one else on this earth that has your unique abilities and gifts. You have the right to express those gifts with imperfection. You get to learn as you grow. You don't have to do it perfectly; you just have to keep going.

Keep growing to that greater, fuller, more authentic expression of who you TRULY are, at the core of your being. That beingness in you, that perfectly imperfect, flawed, brilliant you, that IS God. The unique expression that only you can be. The one that deserves to experience unconditional love, even when you mess up. Even when you make mistakes. Even when you straight-up SCREW UP. You still deserve unconditional love. Just because.

I don't want you to just dance to the beat of your own drum, I want you to dance to the beat of your own band, your own SYMPHONY! Celebrate you like never before. The unique expression of you that **only** you can be. Celebrate the flawed you, the perfect imperfections, the neuroses, the idiosyncrasies, the things that drive people utterly crazy about you, the darkest parts of you. Even the dark parts that you are too ashamed to share with the rest of the world. Even with all of that, you **still** deserve to be UNCONDITIONALLY LOVED, most especially by yourself.

Today is the day to begin to let go of the woundedness, the victim in you and the voices in your head that tell you that you are not enough, not worthy, or not capable. They are old beliefs that no longer serve you, and are based on earlier life experiences or someone else's opinion of you. There is no truth to them. Choose a new belief that **you are worthy, you are capable and you DO deserve.**

Research professor, five-time bestselling author, and shame and vulnerability expert Brené Brown shares, *"Imperfections are not inadequacies; they are reminders that we're all in this together."* When you begin to let go of the beliefs that no longer serve you, you step into a new way of being. When you no longer tolerate gossip, negativity, put-downs, or being someone else's emotional punching-bag within yourself, then you will no longer allow those actions from others. You will set and maintain boundaries that are worthy of you. **The world will take your lead.**

Teach others how to treat you by how you treat yourself. If you want to be treated like you are worthy, beautiful, valuable, and capable, start treating yourself that way and notice how the world changes around you.

The F-Word

Forgiveness. The "F" word. Many of us fear this word, though forgiveness is often misunderstood from the perspective of what it is, what it is not, who it is for, and what the intention behind it is. We often think of forgiveness as letting go of a hurt, "forgiving and forgetting," or we think of it as being for the other person. None of these is actually what forgiveness is really about.

Forgiveness is about making peace with your past. It is not accepting WHAT (whatever hurt) happened, but it **is** about accepting THAT it happened. You cannot change it but you can CHOOSE to no longer LIVE in it. Forgiveness is honoring that whatever happened, happened, recognizing how it has impacted your life, and then choosing to make peace with it and let it go.

Forgiveness is NOT about absolving responsibility, letting someone off the hook who should be held accountable for their actions, or pretending that nothing ever happened. Practicing forgiveness is not even about the other person.

When we hold on to old hurts and resentments, it's like drinking poison and waiting for the other person to die. They are going about their lives, unaffected by the resentment **we** carry within ourselves. It doesn't do anything to harm them. Holding on to the hurt does, though, wear a hole in **your** soul, like a cancer eating you from the inside out. Holding on to that pain and hurt will only cause you to experience more pain and hurt.

Even more than that, if someone caused harm to you or hurt you so badly, why would you want to continue to give them power over your life by letting them take up space in your head and your heart **rent-free?** The BEST revenge for a hurt that someone caused you is to go about living your **best** life with joy, peace, and abundance. That is the ultimate revenge for a wrong that has been done to you.

One of the clients that I worked with, Rachel, was a woman in her mid-40's who had been the victim of sexual abuse by her older brother for several years, beginning at the age of five. She carried deep, deep resentment toward her brother for nearly 40 years. It manifested through mental health issues, weight gain, sleeplessness, nightmares, and extreme anxiety. After just a few sessions using powerful techniques to facilitate forgiveness, Rachel was able to release the resentment toward her brother. In addition, and perhaps most importantly, she was able to release the shame and guilt that she carried for all those years. She immediately felt lighter. She described it as feeling, "like a weight was lifted from my chest and my heart." She simply could not access the feelings of resentment any longer.

Since that time, the resentment and anger that Rachel had carried for DECADES, did not return. Amazingly, her nightmares stopped, she began sleeping at night, and her anxiety and depression significantly decreased. Rachel, like so many of my clients, was amazed at how quickly this release and transformation took place.

That transformation is the power of understanding the subconscious mind. Even deeply painful wounds, even from as far back as childhood, do NOT require years and years of therapy or reliving the painful experiences in order to gain resolution on them. Today, Rachel is working on becoming a life coach so that she can help facilitate for others the kind of transformation that she experienced. That is the power of forgiveness. It allows you to stand ON your story rather than in your story.

Key #2: Contribution

You are meant for something BIGGER. If you are reading this, if you are breathing, there is a purpose in your being here. **You have a gift that you are meant to share on the planet that only YOU can share.** Out of more than seven billion people on the planet, no one can share your gift in the particular and unique way that you can share it. No one.

Your Gift is in Your Journey

In the process of learning, growing, and evolving, you will find the gift that you are meant to share on the planet. Here's the thing about it. **Your gift is IN your journey.** But until you go through your own **evolution** - your healing and transformation - you can't get to your **contribution** - your life's purpose, the gift that you are meant to share.

How your share your unique gift with the world can take a bazillion and one different ways, but you'll discover that as you journey through your evolution. Your gift might be to lead a spiritual revolution, play music or perform, tend a beautiful garden, invent something that changes people's lives, teach yoga, be the crossing guard who ensures that children are safe, or make people laugh. Your gift might be simply to be the person that makes others light up just by being in your presence. It might be compassion in action.

Getting clarity about your life's purpose and your gift doesn't mean that how you share it in the world never changes. How we share our gift in life can change, grow, and evolve over time, as we change, grow, and evolve. The bottom line though, is that everyone has a gift.

Find Your Joy, Find Your Purpose

Joy is the experience that tells us when we are in alignment, when we are where we are supposed to be. If you are doing something that doesn't bring you joy, **do something else**. Take action to do a course correction and fix what needs to be fixed.

Find what brings you joy! What lights you up, gets you excited to get up in the morning, and makes you get lost in it? Do THAT thing more. Your joy is your guidance. Find what brings you joy, what causes a fire in your belly.

When you find that gift, go for it! Live your life FULL-OUT. Be bold enough to answer that calling. Live your dreams! Jack Canfield, personal development leader and originator of the *Chicken Soup for the Soul* series, says that, "Joy is your guidance system." If what you do does not bring you joy, CHANGE it. If a relationship that you are in does not bring you joy, do the work to fix it. If the career or job you have drains the life out of you, make a course correction. If the way that you are living your life today does not bring you joy, make a shift. JOY is your guidance system.

Live Your Legacy, Leave Your Legacy

When you do your own inner work and heal that which needs to be healed, the way in which you are meant to share your purpose will simply manifest itself. Once you gain healing and resolution in your own life, you can focus outwardly and see opportunities to share your gifts, talents, and passions with the world. When you do that, you leave a powerful legacy.

What is your "why"? What do you want to be remembered for? What kind of world do you want to leave behind for future generations? How can you BE that legacy, now? How can you share your gifts and talents such that they impact the world in a positive way?

Everyone is meant to fulfill their purpose. But here's the truth: we all have the **same ultimate purpose**, which is to learn, grow, and evolve into our highest and greatest selves. THAT is our one true purpose in life. That is our highest legacy.

What are you here to do? What gifts have you been given that you are not yet sharing? What makes you feel passionate? What do you get so fired up about that, when you dream about living life doing that thing, you can't sleep? What sets your soul on fire? Find THAT.

Give. Connect. Serve. Choose love, because love is all there is. **We are simply here to practice love.** Love for ourselves, love for each other, love for humanity, and love for the earth.

Love is the answer.

Key #3: Live Each Day JOYfully

Choose Joy

Have a practice of upliftment and connection. Meditate. Sit in stillness. Watch Oprah's SuperSoul Sunday. Read books that challenge your perceptions and raise your consciousness. Get connected with nature. Serve, not for the purpose of gaining some sort of validation or acknowledgment, but simply to be in service. Being in true, authentic service is the ultimate goal in spiritual growth.

Listen to uplifting music. Music feeds the soul; it can literally change our brains on a molecular level by changing the frequency of the brain waves. It is a form of meditation. Music heals. My good friend and Grammy award-winning blues artist Keb' Mo' sets an intention when he records his albums that his music will work to heal people. It absolutely does.

Stop making your busy-ness and all of the people you love and take care of in your life an excuse not to take action on your own life because **they're the exact reason that you *need* to.** Stop postponing your life and your dreams. Reclaim your life and your JOY!

Start NOW, because today is all we have. No matter how shitty you might feel some days, own it. Living each day joyfully doesn't mean that life is all rainbows and butterflies; it simply means that you choose to see your life through the lens of gratitude and opportunities to grow and evolve, even on the challenging days. Embrace your perfect imperfections, right where you are, and MOVE. Take action!

You don't need to know how. You don't need to have all the answers. You don't need to be "ready." Simply CHOOSE and MOVE. Take the first step. The Universe is constantly conspiring for your highest and greatest good. It is on your side. When you choose YOU, the Universe will respond in kind. It will provide for you.

Live with Intention

How does it look to live life with clear intention and urgency? Simply make a **decision** to work on being a better version of yourself every day. Find your authentic, genuine self. Who you truly are. Unapologetically. Look in the mirror and say to yourself, "I love you. You're a badass." You cannot give more love to others than you give to yourself. You cannot let in more love from others than you give to yourself.

Be in relationship with people that support you on your journey. Look at the five people you spend the most time with in your life. It's been said that you are the sum total of the five people you spend the most time with and the books that you read. What kind of books are you reading and who do you surround yourself with?

Have a practice every evening of giving appreciation for the blessings of your day. Visualize your goals for the next day. Whatever you think, read, or talk about before you go to bed is what you will tend to manifest the next day.

That's why sleeping with the TV on is a really unhealthy habit. Your unconscious mind takes in whatever it hears on the TV. Because we are vibrational beings, we reflect the vibration that we surround ourselves with and immerse ourselves in, back out into the Universe. In turn, we attract more of that vibration to us. If you fall asleep listening to whatever is on the TV all night, whether it is the news, violent shows, or reality dramas, you will match that vibration, reflect it back out, and continue to attract more of the same vibration back to you.

Have a daily practice of honestly assessing how you show up in your own life and in the world. Ask yourself reflective questions. Where could I have been more loving today? Where could I take more responsibility? How could I have made today better? Ask yourself not what you are doing, but who you are BEing in the world. Are you the kind of person that lifts others up? Are you someone who brings joy to the world? Do you practice kindness, compassion, and empathy?

This is your time to make a choice about where you move in your life from this day forward. You can either choose to continue to do the same as you've always done, and get exactly what you've always had. You can choose to continue in discontent; a lack of joy, peace, or fulfillment; unhappy relationships; not knowing your purpose; or not feeling excited to get out of bed in the morning. Or, you can choose to take steps to **create the life that you TRULY desire and deserve.**

It is your time to dance. It is your time to sing your song. It is your time to let your light shine.

Let yourself be seen.

Live WITH purpose, ON purpose.

Practice Gratitude

One of the simplest, yet most powerful daily practices that will **profoundly change your life**, is a practice of gratitude. When you intentionally have gratitude for the gifts in your life, you will begin to FIND MORE to be thankful for. David Steindl-Rast, a benedictine monk who meditates and writes on the gentle power of gratitude, teaches that *"It is not joy that makes us grateful; it is gratitude that makes us joyful."*

Start and end each day by listing three things that you are grateful for. When you start each day this way, it sets the tone for the day ahead and you will find that you approach the entire day looking through a different lens. When you end each day this way, you get restful sleep that is focused on what you have to be grateful for rather than on worry, doubt, fear, lack, or limitation.

Every day, find some way to practice gratitude. Focus your attention and look for things that bring you joy or that you are grateful for. I challenge you to give the practice of gratitude a week; you'll notice that you feel happier, fuller, more grateful, and more joyful about your life, regardless of the circumstances.

I want to challenge you, right now, to email me at deanne@deanne-joy.com THREE THINGS that you're grateful for! Be sure to tell me you're reading the book so I can celebrate your win with you! These are the small steps that are within our control every day. And it's important to celebrate those wins.

No Regrets

This book, and my mission, isn't just about wanting you to explore end-of-life values and complete advance directives. Yes, those are important (and I want you to read this book to the end and take ACTION on completing YOUR advance directive). But my larger mission is about that AND so much more.

I invite you to join your life, to live your life in such a way that you are FILLED FULL and FULFILLED, so that, whenever your time comes to leave this physical world, you can look back on your life with **no regrets**. I want you to know that you played full-out, went for your dreams, had deeply connected relationships, did what your heart longed for, and left an imprint on the planet.

I invite you to ask the hard questions and search for the deeper answers. Who ARE you? What do you want, REALLY? What does your heart long for? What brings you so much joy, that, when you are doing it, you completely lose track of time? How do you want to be remembered by your family/friends/community when you are no longer in this physical world with them? What is the gift that you were put here to share?

When I leave this physical world, I want to know that I made a contribution, that I loved deeply, used the gifts and talents that I was given for good, and that I went like gangbusters for my dreams. What dreams do **you** have? What is the passion that burns inside of you, that you have always wanted to do? What have you put on the back burner in order to focus on others, family, or career?

Now is the time to resurrect those dreams. Now is the time to take action. Now is the time to say, "I deserve it, I am capable, and I am going for it." Author Napoleon Hill said it best when he wrote, "Whatever the mind can conceive and believe, it can achieve."

Don't let anyone steal your joy. A word of caution as you embark on a journey of up-leveling your life. Not everyone will join you in your newfound vision of yourself and the world around you. Even people that are closest to you may resist it when you begin to make positive changes in your life. We resist change when we fear the unknown. Don't let others steal your joy. Don't let them bring you back to a place of hiding so the rest of the world can't see you.

If they don't want to join you on your journey of growth and evolution, that's up to them. You can still love them and decide how you want them to be in your life. You can set boundaries so that their negativity or resistance to your growth doesn't set you back. Surround yourself with people that are on their own journey of growth and who will hold you to a higher standard than you hold yourself.

If you don't invest in your own life, who will? Start taking action TODAY to create the life you desire and deserve. No more complaining, wishing, hoping, or complacency. Choose. Make a decision to stop postponing your life or settling for less than you deserve and are capable of. Choose something more. You deserve it.

Take the first step, and then take the next. What is one action step that you can take TODAY toward what you want? I've given you a whole list of actionable tools that you can start using now. Put one foot in front of the other and take a step. Just one. Then take the next one. Success builds on success. Start small, but START.

Do Your Work. We all have our own journey and our own work to do on ourselves. Be willing to take on that journey; to gain resolution on past experiences that hold you back, to stop playing small, and to step into a more powerful version of yourself. If you need help or support, ask for it.

If you put these keys into practice, you will begin to experience your life through an entirely different lens and feel that confidence, clarity, and peace that you want and deserve.

Making a change isn't always easy, but it is simple. This is not rocket science; it is clear and understandable. It's easy to overcomplicate things, when it really just takes focusing on simple, yet powerful practices consistently.

Take action today to create the life you desire because tomorrow isn't promised. I don't want to look back on my life with regrets, do you?

I didn't think so. You're way too powerful for that.

You've got this.

PART IV

THE LAST LOVE LETTER

Understanding Advance Care Planning

In the process of exploring living and dying in my career and personal life, I also became somewhat of an expert and a huge proponent of advance directives. My mission in writing this book and speaking and coaching on this topic is to create an honest, open, societal conversation around death and dying. My hope is to motivate you to take action on completing your advance directive and to encourage, motivate, and inspire you to live your life fully TODAY because tomorrow simply isn't promised. Life is meant to be lived NOW. Hopefully this book provides you with a place to start.

I included this section about advance care planning and healthcare advance directives to help you begin to consider your values and wishes and to TAKE ACTION to complete your directive. Exploring your values, making your wishes known, and putting them in writing ensures that your wishes will be honored and that your loved ones will never be faced with the burden of making those difficult decisions on your behalf.

Making healthcare decisions for yourself or someone who is no longer able to do so can be overwhelming. That's why it's important to get a clear idea about preferences and arrangements while you can make decisions and participate in planning. Advance care planning is the process of making decisions about the care you want to receive if you are ever unable to speak for yourself.[1]

These decisions are yours to make, regardless of what you choose for your care, and the decisions are based on your personal values, preferences, and discussions with your care provider and loved ones. Advance care planning is NOT just for the aging or elderly. A medical crisis can happen at any age, at any time. Both of my parents died suddenly and unexpectedly, my father at the age of 39, my mother at the age of 68. I completed my advance directive when I was pregnant with my daughter.

Though it might make life easier, we don't have a crystal ball to tell us when we will die and we aren't born with an expiration date stamped on the bottoms of our feet. Therefore, it is important to learn about and understand the types of decisions that might need to be made if you became unable to speak for yourself. It is essential to thoroughly consider those decisions ahead of time, and then make your wishes known by talking about them with your loved ones and completing your healthcare advance directive. This is not a morbid thing to contemplate. Rather, it is about taking your ENTIRE life into your own hands, determining how you want to experience your complete journey in this physical world, AND how you want your loved ones to experience your complete journey through your life AND death.

What is a Healthcare Advance Directive?

A healthcare advance directive is a legal document describing your wishes for your medical care should you ever become incapacitated or unable to speak for yourself. Completing an advance directive allows one to leave very specific instructions about decisions such as being revived; receiving cardiopulmonary resuscitation (CPR); having a breathing tube, breathing machine, or feeding tubes;

having invasive medical procedures; or dealing with issues like quality-of-life.

A healthcare advance directive is a legal document that **goes into effect <u>only</u> if or when you become disabled and unable to speak for yourself.** This could be the result of disease or severe injury—no matter how old you are. An advance directive helps others know what type of medical care you want. It also allows you to express your values and desires related to end-of-life care.[2] More importantly, it gives your loved ones the gift of peace, clarity, and healing at a time when they most need it. You can change or adjust it at any time, as your health or life circumstances change.

It is absolutely NOT necessary to hire an attorney or go to court to complete an advance directive. It is a relatively simple process that you can complete on your own or with your healthcare provider. Each state may have slightly different laws and guidelines around advance directives, so I encourage you to explore your state's standards for these documents. The National Hospice and Palliative Care Organization also provides free advance directives and instructions for each state as a PDF on their website http://caringinfo.org.

My absolute favorite healthcare advance directive form, and the one that I recommend to all of my clients, friends, and family, is called Five Wishes.[3] Not only is the document easy-to-understand and very user-friendly, but it is beautifully written and helps to facilitate discussion and explore your values and wishes in a dignified and life-affirming way. The Five Wishes document is written in everyday language and helps you express your wishes in areas that matter most — the personal and spiritual in addition to the medical and legal. It also helps you describe what good care means to you, whether you are seriously ill or not.

I've always said that my mom was the poster child for how to prepare an advance directive. Everything that she knew to make sure was in her directive was handwritten. When she completed hers more than a decade ago, most advance directive forms didn't include personal and spiritual matters or describing what good care means to you. The

Five Wishes form is now readily available and addresses all of the things that, as a geriatric nurse, my mom knew to include, but the average person would not. I cannot recommend it highly enough. This document allows you to see the beauty in the full circle of life, in an uplifting, healing, and life-affirming way. And, most importantly, it is simple and straightforward.

The last page of the Five Wishes document notes each state that has unique guidelines or requirements. Even if your state does not honor the Five Wishes form (there are only a handful that do not), it can certainly be an addendum attached to the legal document for your state. You can find the Five Wishes guide online at http://fivewishes.org.

Generally speaking, all you need to formalize an advance directive is to either have it signed by two witnesses, who cannot be care providers, blood relatives, or named as your durable power of attorney for healthcare, or have it notarized by a notary public. Then, keep a copy with all of your important documents (not in a safe deposit box, but somewhere that it is accessible), and give one to your healthcare provider, one to your area hospital, and one to the people closest to you.

Peace of Mind

Even if we talk with our loved ones about what our wishes, values, and beliefs around the end of life might be, what I have found over the decades of working with the dying and those closest to them is that at the moment of facing the death of a loved one, it is very difficult for many people to make decisions about letting them go. I frequently found this to be the case even if they had direct conversations about these choices or if there was little chance for meaningful recovery.

Often, those conversations about end-of-life decisions are had in the form of hypothetical situations that we could never fathom actually happening to us or our loved ones. We see a program on television that shows someone in a coma, on life support, or paralyzed and on a ventilator following an accident, and say to our spouse, half in jest,

"If I'm ever like that, please just pull the plug." But that's often as far as the conversation goes - a vague hypothetical, not very likely to occur in that particular manner. Even when conversations are more direct and one's choices are made very clear, there remains such an element of guilt and questioning. We continue to wonder whether or not we're doing the "right thing," doing "enough" to give our loved ones a chance, or truly speaking to our loved one's wishes versus our own. This includes exploring whether there is a difference between extending life and having a **quality of life.**

A healthcare advance directive allows for that burden to be lifted from loved ones, so that they can focus on their own mourning and grief, rather than be burdened with decisions that are very difficult to make in that frame of mind. However, it is NOT enough to simply complete an advance directive. It is absolutely **essential** to have conversations with loved ones and those that will be left to carry out the wishes expressed in the directive. In my transformational coaching programs, we actually focus on this for an entire module, and I walk you through the entire process, from exploring your values and wishes, to completing your advance directive, to having conversations with your loved ones.

It is essential that the loved ones of the person dying MUST understand and be comfortable with sharing with healthcare providers the wishes expressed in the directive. At the time of facing that potential loss, it is often extremely difficult and painful for families to let go, even when their loved one's wishes have been made clear in an advance directive. Grief is one of the most difficult emotions for many people to experience. It makes us vulnerable, and many of us are terribly afraid of being vulnerable. In my experience working with thousands of families over the years, grief can amplify both our strengths and our weaknesses. In other words, grief can bring out the healthiest and the most dysfunctional nature of individuals, as well as families.

I've seen grief bring families much closer together to experience a strength and bonding that they didn't previously have. I have also seen grief tear families apart and significantly magnify the dysfunction that may have existed previously, even under the radar. Add to that difficulty the burden of making decisions on behalf of a loved one in the absence of an advance directive, and it can irreparably fracture a family. I have experienced far too many families that were never able to recover from the strain of stark divisions in the process of making difficult end-of-life decisions on behalf of a loved one who had not completed an advance directive or included their family in end-of-life conversations. It is a tragedy that compounds an already-difficult loss.

When patients know that their wishes have been decided in advance, that they will be honored because they are written in a formal document, and they have had conversations with their loved ones, it provides a relief and a peace at the end of life that is an incredible gift to them and their loved ones. A healthcare advance directive takes that weight off of the family's shoulders that can sometimes lead to discord, fear, and disconnect when they are left to make decisions on their loved ones' behalf with no direction. In many cases, including my own personal experience, an advance directive allows loved ones to focus on simply being present in love and peace, rather than in fear and guilt. It can be the most profound final gift one can leave their loved ones.

As many as 80% of Americans express that they want to die at home[4], yet two out of three have not completed an advance directive.[5] Approximately 75% of older adults die in hospitals and nursing homes. The majority of money that is spent on care for older adults is spent in the last year, often in the last months of life.[6] There is incongruence between what people say that they want at the end of their lives and what actually happens. Modern medicine is a magnificent thing, yet there needs to be a larger conversation around what is appropriate and in alignment with one's values and wishes versus doing everything medically possible just because we have the technology to do it.

In considering treatment decisions, your personal values are key. Is your main desire to have the most days of life or to have the most life in your days? What if an illness leaves you paralyzed or in a permanent coma and you need to be on a ventilator? Would you want that? What makes life meaningful to you?

You might want doctors to try CPR if your heart stops or to use a ventilator for a short time if you have trouble breathing, if that means that there is a possibility in the future that you could be well enough to spend time with your family. Even if the emergency leaves you simply able to spend your days listening to books on audio or gazing out the window, watching the birds and squirrels compete for seeds in the bird feeder, you might be content with that. If not, then it's an even more important consideration when it comes to making decisions about your healthcare treatment. This is the kind of open, ongoing dialogue that needs to take place with your healthcare providers and loved ones, not just when you become ill.

The baby boomer generation has seen their parents age in a society capable of keeping people alive for longer and longer as medicine advances. My sincere hope is that this aging generation will push forward the conversation about choice at the end of life and the importance of openly discussing quality of life, values, and wishes, rather than simply pursuing all available aggressive treatments, simply because we can.

Healthcare Power of Attorney

A healthcare power of attorney (POA) is a proxy, or surrogate, that you appoint to make decisions on your behalf, should you become unable to do so.[7] It is important that your proxy understand your values and wishes, and that they feel comfortable expressing those wishes on your behalf, even in the face of crisis or grief. If they are not comfortable doing so, they are not the best person to serve as your POA. Comfort in speaking on your behalf and ensuring that your wishes are honored is EXTREMELY important and should be a primary consideration when appointing a POA. You can appoint a POA in addition to or instead of an advance directive.

While I believe that we are never too young to complete an advance directive and explore our end-of-life wishes, a POA can help you be prepared for unforeseen situations, like a serious accident. The Five Wishes document mentioned previously includes appointing a healthcare power of attorney.

CPR and DNR

It is important for you to understand basic terminology related to advance healthcare planning so that you can make informed decisions about your healthcare wishes. If you don't understand something, ASK your provider to explain it to you. Write down your questions so that you don't forget them the next time you meet with your healthcare team. Your job is to make sure that you know and understand all of the information you need to make informed decisions about your own care.

CPR (Cardiopulmonary Resuscitation)

CPR stands for cardiopulmonary resuscitation. It is an emergency life-saving procedure that is done when someone's breathing or heartbeat has stopped. This may happen after an electric shock, heart attack, or drowning. Yet CPR is an invasive and traumatic procedure, often resulting in bruising, broken ribs, and the risk of not surviving the intensive care that follows.

Emergency resuscitation measures may also involve electric shocks and emergency medications to help keep blood moving to essential organs while stabilizing. **Heroic measures** include all invasive procedures to attempt to revive or resuscitate a person such as CPR, electric shocks, life support, or a breathing machine.[8]

DNR (Do Not Resuscitate) Order

A do-not-resuscitate order, or DNR order, is a medical order written by a doctor. It instructs health care providers not to do cardiopulmonary resuscitation (CPR) if a patient's breathing stops or if the patient's heart stops beating. A DNR order allows you to choose whether or not you want CPR in an emergency. It is specific about CPR. It does not have instructions for other treatments, such as pain medicine, other medicines, or nutrition.

DNR means that, if your heart stops, or you stop breathing, you do NOT want to be brought back to life via CPR or by having a tube stuck down your throat (intubation) and attached to a ventilator (breathing machine).

DNR does NOT mean *Do Not Treat*

Just because you may not want the 'heroic measures' of CPR or breathing machines, there's much that can be done for care and comfort. DNR does NOT mean 'do not care for this patient.'

Asking for a DNR order does not mean that care or treatment will be stopped. CPR is a life-saving measure; in other words, if resuscitation is attempted and there does not appear to be a significant chance for meaningful recovery, it can be stopped.

Full Code means that you want all interventions and heroic measures taken should you stop breathing or your heart stop beating.[9]

It is really important to make these decisions educated with accurate information and based on current circumstances, not based on misinformation or prior life experiences. For instance, if you had a parent that experienced a stroke or heart attack, underwent CPR, and ultimately did not survive, you may decide that "I don't ever want to die like that; just let me die if my heart stops."

But let's say, as in the case of my good friend's husband, that you're an otherwise healthy 46-year-old with young children and a family that needs you, and you experienced a sudden heart attack with no prior evidence of risk factors. Your youth, health, and immediate medical intervention enhance the chances of you surviving and recovering from this heart attack, and going on to have a full, healthy life so you can watch your children grow up and become parents themselves.

Because my friend's husband had seen his own parent go through serious health problems and ultimately not recover, he decided that under NO circumstances did he want to undergo CPR. Fortunately for him, he didn't have it in writing when he suffered a massive heart attack at 46, and his wife made the decision to do everything that could be done for him. In the end, he fully recovered. And he was clearly grateful that she made that decision on his behalf. Had she not, even though there was a good chance that he could have fully recovered, he would have lost that opportunity - and so would his loved ones, including his two young children.

The point is, these decisions should not be made in a vacuum; they can change as your situation and health circumstances change. If you had Stage-4 brain cancer or some other terminal illness, your considerations about CPR might be significantly different than those of someone who is a healthy 46-year-old with no significant health history. In other words, these decisions are not black and white decisions; they are very much based on your current situation, your life experiences, beliefs, values, desires, etc. There is no right or wrong.

Palliative Care vs. Hospice

Palliative Care and Hospice are two of the greatest gifts in medicine for those who are facing serious or life-limiting illnesses and their loved ones.

Palliative care (pronounced pal-lee-uh-tiv) is specialized medical care for people with serious illness. It focuses on providing relief from the symptoms and stress of a serious illness. The goal is to improve quality of life for both the patient and the family. It is provided by a specially-trained team of doctors, nurses, social workers, and other specialists who work together with a patient's doctors to provide an extra layer of support. It is appropriate at any age and at any stage in a serious illness and can be provided along with curative treatment. One can receive palliative care, for instance, at the same time that they are undergoing aggressive chemo and radiation for cancer.

Hospice care is intended to provide comfort to you and your family during a life-limiting illness, rather than provide treatments to cure the illness. **Comfort care** is an essential part of medical care at the end of life. It is care that helps or soothes a person who is dying. The goals are to prevent or relieve suffering as much as possible and to improve quality of life while respecting the dying person's wishes.

Palliative care is similar to comfort care in hospice, but it is offered along with any medical treatments you might receive for a life-threatening illness, such as chemotherapy for cancer or dialysis for kidney failure. The main goal of both hospice and palliative care is to keep you comfortable. In addition, you can always choose to move from hospice to palliative care if you want to pursue treatments to cure your illness.

Hospice is for patients who have a terminal or life-limiting illness, typically with a life expectancy of six-months to a year. With hospice, treatment shifts from aggressively pursuing a cure to keeping the patient comfortable and giving them a quality of life for whatever time they have remaining. Hospice can happen at home, in a hospital, in a nursing home, or in an inpatient hospice program. Any time that a patient is no longer receiving treatment to CURE an illness, such as advanced cancer that is no longer treatable or has not responded to aggressive interventions, hospice can play an integral role in providing the support and care needed to maintain quality of life. One can be in palliative care, for instance, and choose to transition to hospice care if their illness progresses and they decide to no longer pursue curative treatments.[10]

Palliative care and hospice have come a long way in terms of the mainstream understanding of the incredibly important role that they play in patient care. However, they are still highly under-utilized, and their value is greatly underappreciated. In my experience working in end-of-life care, I have found that, too often, patients are referred to palliative care or hospice when they are actively dying, or at the end stages of life. However, palliative care can be used at any time, not just for terminal illnesses.

Too often, hospice is brought in only when a patient has progressed past a certain point in the dying process. However, hospice can be brought in much sooner in that process, up to a year before, to provide physician and nursing care, pastoral care, and a social worker. Hospice provides care for the whole person, physical, emotional, and spiritual, as well as for the family of the patient.

It is terribly underutilized, in part because of that collective fear of talking about death that I discussed earlier, and in part because it is not explained and explored openly with primary care providers BEFORE it is needed. Yet, it is an amazing service and provides such value, and can truly assist patients and their loved ones in experiencing a peaceful death. Hopefully, as palliative care and hospice become more and more mainstream, their utilization will continue to grow so that they are used to their fullest benefits. I simply cannot overstate the incredible gifts that both palliative and hospice care offer during a serious or life-limiting illness.

A Liberating Decision

Using death as your gauge for how you live life TODAY is core to truly owning and activating your best life, and preparing for the inevitable. Dying doesn't have to be scary. Talking about what is TRULY important to us, what we want in the event that we become too ill or incapacitated to speak for ourselves, and what our end-of-life values and wishes are can be both empowering and liberating. Beyond preparing for the inevitable, there is a certain gift in talking about our own mortality. It creates a sense of purpose and urgency in how we live our lives NOW. It can give us the opportunity to really consider whether we are living fully today - being present, making memories, sharing our gifts and passions, creating our own legacy - knowing that tomorrow isn't promised.

Our job is to live a fulfilled and joyful life, so that we can have a peaceful death, whenever that time comes. Completing our advance directive prepares us and our loved ones for the inevitable, gives us the opportunity to take charge of our future, and allows us to be fully present in our lives today as we choose to live each day boldly. It ensures that our wishes will be honored and that our loved ones will never have to carry the burden of making those difficult decisions on our behalf. Do yourself and your loved ones the honor of giving that gift of an advance directive.

Do it Today.

The Last Love Letter

My mother shared my love and passion for being with and working with patients and their loved ones at the end of life. Like me, she saw this work as the greatest honor, privilege, and gift. She felt as strongly as I did about the importance of completing advance directives and preparing for the inevitable by making one's wishes known, while fully embracing life each moment. I continue to feel, as I did then, that it is part of my mother's legacy to share the importance of completing an advance directive.

By completing hers, my mom gave us the most beautiful, profound gift - her last love letter to us, in the form of her advance directive. Through it, she spoke directly to my siblings and me. Every decision that needed to be made was already made. Any fear, guilt, reservation, or second-guessing that we might have had, was completely removed after reading her directive. She removed the weight of making profoundly difficult decisions from our shoulders, which allowed us to simply BE with her and with each other, as we said goodbye and released her.

The gift that my mom gave my siblings and me will forever change our memories and experience of her death. It was a deeply spiritual experience. As difficult and painful as the circumstances leading to her death were, hers truly was a "good death." As beautiful a death as I have ever experienced. I was honored to be with her and to release her to her next beyond, peacefully, lovingly, beautifully. That moment will forever be with me. It was an experience that touched me deeply and profoundly. It brought with it a deep, deep healing, gratitude, and clarity.

Her death is, quite literally, what led me to write this book and do this work, so that others can experience the same peace, love, presence, and freedom in releasing their loved ones to their next beyond. My mom's last gift to us was the most profound and life-changing gift that she could have ever given. That is the power of an advance directive. That is the power of presence, vulnerability, authentically being in the moment, and embracing the reality and beauty of life and death.

That is the power of LOVE.

The following is a final thought by one of my favorite spiritual thought leaders, best-selling author Marianne Williamson. This passage perfectly sums up the intention behind this book and my work.

OUR DEEPEST FEAR

By

Marianne Williamson

Our deepest fear is not that we are inadequate. Our deepest fear is that we are powerful beyond measure. It is our light, not our darkness that most frightens us. We ask ourselves, who am I to be brilliant, gorgeous, talented, fabulous? Actually, who are you not to be? You are a child of God. Your playing small does not serve the world. There is nothing enlightened about shrinking so that other people won't feel insecure around you. We are all meant to shine, as children do. We were born to make manifest the glory of God that is within us. It's not just in some of us; it's in everyone. And as we let our own light shine, we unconsciously give other people permission to do the same. As we are liberated from our own fear, our presence automatically liberates others.

NEXT STEPS

So, where do you go from here? What do you want to do next? My strong invitation to you would be to KEEP MOVING. I don't want you to just read this book, feel good, be inspired, but then not do anything with it. The way to keep moving forward is to simply START. Take action on what you've learned in this book. Start implementing it - today.

There are several options for you to continue on this journey that you've begun and build on your momentum:

OPTION #1: JOIN MY TRIBE

If you are a woman in midlife and you'd like to join a vibrant community of other powerful, deserving women from around the world, JUST LIKE YOU, who are all committed to their own journey of healing and transformation - join my Choose Joy tribe in my free private Facebook group. You can find it at facebook.com/groups/choosejoygroup.

OPTION #2: DIG DEEPER INTO THE WORK

If you have loved what you've learned here and you know that you want to continue on this journey that you've started beyond the pages of this book, but you're not quite sure yet what the next best step is for you, schedule a complimentary discovery session and let's explore where you want to be, consider some options, and get you a clear plan of action to build on what you've begun here. You can schedule that session at deannejoy.as.me/discovery-session.

OPTION #3: EXPERIENCE A FREE MIDLIFE REBOOT BREAKTHROUGH SESSION

If reading this book has you curious about working with me and you'd like to experience coaching with me first-hand, take advantage of my free 30-minute *Midlife Reboot Breakthrough Session.* I'll lead you through a powerful process for experiencing breakthrough and gaining resolution in an area of your life that you are feeling stuck in, and you'll leave with clear action steps to build on the momentum that you've gained. You can schedule that at deannejoy.as.me/free-intro-session.

OPTION #4: WORK WITH ME

If you'd like to work directly with me to begin diving in and applying these tools either in my signature group coaching experience *Ultimate Midlife Reboot : Living with No Regrets^{TM}* or in my 1:1 private coaching and mentorship programs, we will take a DEEP DIVE into the full spectrum of the tools that I teach (this book is about the size of my pinky in comparison to the goods that you'll get in my signature programs). You can find out more about working with me through my coaching programs at deanne-joy.com/work-with-me.

OPTION #5: DIVE INTO MY FREE VIDEO MINI-COURSE

If you know that you've gotten a ton out of the book, one way to ensure that you STAY IN ACTION is to check out my free video mini-course, *3 Keys to Discovering YOU in Midlife* .

You can find it at deanne-joy.com/3-keys-book-gift/.

Whatever you decide is the next best step for you, here's the important thing. TAKE A STEP. Stay in action. Don't stay stuck. Implement what you've learned here right away while it's fresh in your mind, before life gets you distracted once again from really focusing on YOU learning, growing, and evolving into the next iteration of your badass, unstoppable self!

I'd love to hear your feedback about this book, how it resonated with you, and how I can support you in continuing on your journey. Shoot me an email at deanne@deanne-joy.com!

If you're the social media type, I'd love to connect with you! You can find me at:

Facebook - DeAnne Joy - Transformation Coach

Instagram - deannejoy1

YouTube - DeAnne Joy International

Linked In - linkedin.com/in/deanne-joy

Twitter - Coach_DeAnneJoy

Website - deanne-joy.com

EPILOGUE

My genuine hope is that this book has opened your eyes to new possibilities and inspired you to take action to create the life that you TRULY want and deserve. I have poured my heart and soul into it. If you have found value in it, then I ask that you take the following three actions, which would be the greatest gift that you could give me, and my mother through me.

First, complete your own advance directive. Make your own end-of-life wishes known. Do it today. If you need guidance or are interested in taking a deeper dive to learn more about living your legacy and leaving your legacy, then I invite you to schedule a free Midlife Reboot Breakthrough Session with me. You can do that at deannejoy.as.me/free-intro-session.

Second, share this information with those you love and ask them to read it and complete their own advance directives. Engage in conversation with friends and loved ones around the topic. Hopefully this book has provoked thoughts about how to discuss the topics of death and advance care planning from an uplifting, life-affirming perspective that is focused more on living EACH day fully, knowing that tomorrow isn't promised. My intention is to inspire a million people to complete their advance directives AND discuss them with their loved ones as a result of reading this book and hearing my message.

Please help me spread the message by leaving a review on Amazon at https://www.amazon.com/dp/1705629342 **or on GoodReads** at goodreads.com/book/show/48762606-the-last-love-letter.

Also, be sure to let me know when you complete your directive!

Third and most importantly, live your life FULL-OUT. Embrace today and every day. Live authentically and BOLDLY, as though it could be your last day.

Because one day, it will be.

ACKNOWLEDGEMENTS

To all of those whose stories are shared in this book, some anonymously, thank you for allowing me to not just share information, but to create a real connection to the lives of the readers of this book. Thank you for the privilege of trusting me to represent your and your loved ones' voices with honor and love. I have no doubt that your stories will change many lives, as they already have.

To all of the patients, clients, and families that I have worked with, learned from, and grown with over the past 25 years. You have taught me more than any books or education could teach me. I honor your journeys.

To my colleague Dr. Charles Braun for helping me to interpret and understand my father's medical records as I tried to piece together what had actually happened at the time of his death so many years earlier.

To those that have helped me learn how to share my story in the most impactful way, in writing, on video, and on stages. You have been my coaches and mentors along this journey and have directly helped me in this process of sharing my message with the world. Vickie Gould, Lisa Nichols, Dack Quigley, Brenda Adelman, Lori Granito, and Brené Brown (Brené doesn't know it **yet**, and we've never met in person, but she's my "if-you-could-have-dinner-with-anyone, who-would-it-be?" person, and I will definitely meet her one day).

To my editor Andrea McCurry, you are not only brilliant, kind, and passionate about your work, but you have the ability to see my writing through my eyes yet make it so that it's actually understandable outside of my head. Not only that, but you had a tremendous undertaking with reining in my tendency to use 350 words when I could have used 18 (like right there), and you did it well.

To Dr. Marwa Kilani, thank you for jumping at the chance to write the foreword for the book. I am so grateful that our paths crossed all those years ago at Holy Cross Medical Center. You are a gifted physician and a brilliant leader. I learned so much from you about how to have candid, dignified, life-affirming conversations about death, and even making your patients laugh in the midst of their tears. You have much to share with the world and I am so glad that I get to witness the amazing work that you continue to do. I welcome the opportunity to partner again ANY TIME!

To all of the friends and family that have supported me along this journey, encouraged me, and rallied me on, I can't thank you enough. My New Game community - y'all know. My lifelong friend and bestie, Robbie Brooks-Moore - I am grateful beyond words for you.

My Choose Joy community and my clients. Every one of you is an amazing, powerful, deserving woman and I am so blessed to have you in my world. Thank you for allowing me to learn from you and to be inspired by your courageous vulnerability every day.

To Dr. Matthew Masters - your kind, generous, caring, and gifted approach to treating people with addictions has and will continue to save many lives. I knew the first day that I walked into your office that I had turned a corner. Thank you for helping me get my life back.

To my siblings Dennis, Donnie, David, and Cate - My sincere hope is that I have shared my experience with losing our parents in a way that honors their lives and their legacies, while also sharing their humanness. I have shared these stories with the intention of touching many lives and inspiring many more to complete their own Last Love Letter. Thank you for always being supportive, even if you haven't agreed with me or quite understood exactly why I do what I do. Thank you for allowing my story to be just that - mine. I realize that we may have different recollections and experiences, and the stories that I share are only my perspective. Thank you for respecting that.

To my husband Sidney. Thank you for your patience and understanding over the past few years as I have taken on this project. You have always been my biggest supporter and you have always seen greatness in me. I am grateful for the years we have spent together and for your partnership.

To my daughter Marielle - I am so proud of the woman you have become. It hasn't always been easy for us, and I have made more than my share of mistakes along my path as a stepmom. But I will always love you, I am incredibly proud of you, and I hope that this book gives you some perspective that perhaps you didn't have before.

To the best Christmas gift ever, my daughter Amaya. Thank you for inspiring me every day to be a better mom than I thought I was capable of being. You challenge me to keep digging deep. And I can't wait for you to keep your promise of writing a book with me once this one goes to best seller. I'm holding you to that! I want you to always know that ANYTHING you want is POSSIBLE if you are open, believe in yourself, and work for it.

To all of the other ancillary people who have been a part of my journey, please forgive me for not mentioning you individually, but the truth is that I am just terrifically blessed with a lot of brilliant, supportive people in my world and I couldn't be more grateful.

Thank you all from the depths of my soul.

ABOUT THE AUTHOR

DeAnne Joy is a leading transformation and legacy expert, coach, and speaker. Also known as *the Midlife Reboot Mentor*™, her superpower is helping driven women in midlife discover joy and peace after a loss or life-changing event. She draws on both her personal experience as well as her 25-year career as a licensed clinical therapist, master NLP and EFT practitioner, and end-of-life social worker.

DeAnne has trained physicians in facilitating end-of-life conversations with patients and their families and is a strong advocate for completing advance healthcare directives to prepare for the future, while fully embracing life today. She is the founder of DeAnne Joy International and lives in Wisconsin with her husband, 10-year-old daughter, and fur-babies Suzy Q and Jackpot.

You can learn more about DeAnne at deanne-joy.com/meet-deanne or book her for your next speaking event or podcast at deanne-joy.com/speaking.

REFERENCES

1) U.S. National Institute on Aging. 2018. Accessed 10/25/18 at https://nia.nih.gov.

2) U.S. National Library of Medicine. Bethesda, MD. 2019. Accessed 4/25/19 at https://medlineplus.gov

3) Aging with Dignity. 2019. Accessed on 12/4/18 at https://fivewishes.org

4) Flory J, Yinong YX, Gurol I, et al. Place of death: US. trends since 1980. Health Aff. 2004; 23: 194–200.

5) Perelman School of Medicine at the University of Pennsylvania. Published study 2017.

6) Hogan C, Lunney J, Gabel J, et al. Medicare beneficiaries' costs of care in the last year of life. 2001; 20:188–195.

7) U.S. National Institute on Aging. Last updated 2018. Accessed on 10/13/18 at https://nia.nih.gov.

8) U.S. National Library of Medicine. Bethesda, MD 2019. Accessed on 10/13/18 at https://medlineplus.gov

9) Arnold R. "Care of dying patients and their families." In: Goldman L, Schafer AI, eds. *Goldman-Cecil Medicine*. 25th ed. Philadelphia, PA: Elsevier Saunders; 2016: chap 3.

10) National Hospice and Palliative Care Organization. Updated 2019. Accessed 3/18/19 at https://nhpco.org

Made in the USA
San Bernardino, CA
19 January 2020